מאמרי
לכה דודי
תרפ"ט ❖ תשי"ד

THE MAJESTIC
B R I D E

מאמרי
לכה דודי
תרפ"ט ❖ תשי"ד

THE MAJESTIC
B R I D E

two chasidic discourses by
Rabbi Yosef Yitzchak Schneersohn
Rabbi Menachem M. Schneerson
זצוקללה"ה נבג"מ זי"ע
of Lubavitch

•

translated and annotated by
Rabbi Ari Sollish
Rabbi Avraham D. Vaisfiche

KEHOT PUBLICATION SOCIETY
770 Eastern Parkway / Brooklyn, New York, 11213

The Majestic Bride

Published and Copyrighted © 2008
Fourth Printing—January 2021
by
Kehot Publication Society
770 Eastern Parkway / Brooklyn, New York 11213
(718) 774-4000 / Fax (718) 774-2718
editor@kehot.com / www.kehot.org

Orders:
291 Kingston Avenue / Brooklyn, New York 11213
(718) 778-0226 / Fax (718) 778-4148
www.kehot.com

4 6 8 10 12 13 11 9 7 5

Library of Congress Record available at: https://lccn.loc.gov/2008276598

ISBN 978-0-8266-0748-5

Manufactured in the United States of America

CONTENTS

PREFACE

We are pleased to present *The Majestic Bride*, two discourses that analyze the deeper, mystical dimension of the wedding ceremony, as part of the acclaimed *Chasidic Heritage Series*.

The first of these discourses was delivered, in 5689 (1928), by Rabbi Yosef Yitzchak Schneersohn, sixth Lubavitcher Rebbe, at the wedding of his daughter, Rebbetzin Chaya Mushka to Rabbi Menachem Mendel Schneerson—Rabbi Yosef Yitzchak's eventual successor.

The second is a discourse delivered by Rabbi Menachem Mendel Schneerson in 5714 (1954) as an exposition on his father-in-law's discourse.

Both discourses open with the words *Lecha dodi likrat kallah*, sung on Friday evenings as a welcome to the Shabbat bride.

Prior to delivering his discourse, Rabbi Yosef Yitzchak related that at a wedding, the souls of the ancestors of the groom and bride arrive from their abode on high to participate in the celebration. The Rebbe added that by delivering a discourse consisting of teachings from his ancestors—each of the previous Chabad-Lubavitch Rebbes—he would be "inviting" them to the wedding.

At a later date, Rabbi Menachem Mendel, having succeeded Rabbi Yosef Yitzchak as the Lubavitcher Rebbe, urged his Chasidim to follow suit in this beautiful custom and recite the discourse at their own wedding celebrations. In this way, a groom could extend an invitation to the souls of the Rebbes and have them present for this special occasion.

As mentioned, in 5714 (1954), the Rebbe delivered an exposition on his father-in-law's discourse. Twenty five years later, in honor of the Rebbe and Rebbetzin's fiftieth wedding anniversary, the Rebbe edited and officially published his discourse. Subsequently, many saw fit to recite this second discourse at their weddings, also as a symbolic invitation to the

Rebbe (and the previous Rebbes) to participate in the celebration.

It is hoped that the current translation, along with the thorough elucidation and introduction, will benefit those who wish to gain better insight into these fundamental treatises.

To further this volume's usability, the Order of the Betrothal and Marriage Blessings from the *Siddur Tehillat Hashem—Annotated Edition* (Kehot 2003) has been added.

Rabbis Ari Sollish and Avraham D. Vaisfiche translated the discourse and added the extensive annotation and commentary. Special thanks are due to *Heichal Menachem's Chasidut Mevoeret* series and to *Sichos in English*, whose respective publications of these discourses aided in the process. Thanks are also due to Rabbis Dovid Olidort and Yosef B. Friedman for their editorial assistance.

Kehot Publication Society

Purim 5768
Brooklyn, New York

Facsimile of original manuscript of *Lecha Dodi 5689* by Rabbi
Yosef Yitzchak Schneersohn

בס״ד. ש״פ תצא, י״ג אלול ה׳תשי״ד.

לכה דודי לקראת כלה פני שבת נקבלה, ומביא כ״ק מו״ח אדמו״ר (מפרדר״א)

שחתן דומה למלך ובכלה ... זה הקב״ה וכלה היא כנס״י,

ובספירות ... הו״ע ז״א ומלכות, דחתן הוא בחי׳ ז״א וכלה היא בחי׳

מל׳. וזהו לכה דודי לקראת כלה פני שבת נקבלה, שהו״ע המשכת ז״א למל׳,

וסדר ההמשכה הוא, אשר תחילה צ״ל ההמשכה חיצונית (מז״א למל׳) שהיא

רק בבחי׳ מקיף, ואח״כ ... ההמשכה פנימית. דכן הוא הסדר בכל השפעה ממשפיע

למקבל, דתחילה צ״ל המשכת המשפיע בבחי׳ חיצונית שלו לבחי׳ חיצונית המקבל,

שעי״ז מתעלה המקבל להיות קרוב למדרי׳ המשפיע, ואח״כ יוכל לקבל המשכה

הפנימית מהמשפיע. ומביא ע״ז ב׳ משלים [מהשפעת רב לתלמיד, ואב המשחק

עם בנו הקטן]. ויש לומר, שכוונתו במשלים אלה היא לא רק להביא דוגמאות

לסדר ההמשכה (שההשפעה חיצונית היא הקדמה להשפעה פנימית), אלא (גם) לבאר

גם העילוי שבב׳ השפעות אלו, דגם ההשפעה חיצונית היא דרגא נעלית ביותר,

ועד ... מההשפעה פנימית. כי ההשפעה חיצונית, שהיא בחי׳ מקיף,

היא למעלה מכלי המקבל (משא״כ ההשפעה פנימית שמתקבלת בכלי המקבל) אמנם

ומ״מ היא רק הקדמה להשפעה פנימית, כי דוקא ע״י השפעה הפנימית מגיעים

לעילוי נעלה יותר (שלמעלה מבחי׳ המקיף). וזהו על כל כבוד חופה שהם ב׳

בחי׳ כבוד, כבוד חתן וכבוד כלה, ... יחוד או״א ויחוד זו״ן. דעם היות

שבחי׳ אור מקיף, מ״מ ידוע ... ביחוד זו״ן (שהוא יחוד פנימי) נמשך

העצם.

והנה המשל הראשון הוא מהשפעת רב לתלמיד, וסדר ההשפעה הוא כמו שארז״ל דמקמי

דפתח להו לרבנן אמר מילתא דבדיחותא/ולבסוף יתיב באימתא ופתח

בשמעתא, דהמילתא דבדיחותא שקודם הלימוד [שהו״ע שיחת חולין של ח״ח שצריכ

לימוד] היא חיצונית בלבד, אמנם השפעה זו היא הקדמה להשפעה פנימית (דפתח

בשמעתא) כי דוקא עי״ז נעשה פתיחת הלב והמוח של התלמיד שיהי׳ כלי לקבלה

להשפעה פנימית. והנה מקור משל זה הוא מאדמו״ר האמצעי בתורת חיים [אלא

שבתו״ח לא הובא זה כמשל להענין דלכה דודי. ובד״ה סוכים לעד פר״ת (המאמר

שאמר כ״ק אדמו״ר מהורש״ב נ״ע ביום הולדתו (כ׳ מ״ח) האחרון בעלמא דין)

INTRODUCTION
AND SUMMARY

INTRODUCTION AND SUMMARY

A mong the works of the Lubavitcher Rebbes, many are the discourses that were delivered and recited at weddings. When celebrating such festive occasions, the joy of the Chasidic Masters issued forth with an expression of their very essence, resulting in profound teachings on the mystical meaning of marriage and the wedding ceremony in particular. Filling entire volumes, these dissertations are known as *Derushei Chatunah* (wedding discourses), and fortunate was the Chasid who witnessed their delivery at these joyous times for the Rebbes and their families.

THE REBBE'S WEDDING

In 5689 (1928), Rabbi Yosef Yitzchak Schneersohn, sixth Lubavitcher Rebbe, celebrated the wedding of his second daughter, Rebbetzin Chaya Mushka, to Rabbi Menachem Mendel Schneerson—Rabbi Yosef Yitzchak's eventual successor.

To mark the occasion, Rabbi Yosef Yitzchak delivered a series of discourses—before, during, and following the wedding ceremony. The discourse delivered at the *Kabbalat Panim* (the ceremony of "welcoming the bride" prior to the *chuppah*) opened with the words *"Lecha Dodi"* (*Come, my Beloved, to meet the bride; let us welcome the Shabbat*), from the famous Friday evening hymn composed by Rabbi Shlomo Halevi Alkabetz, a 16th-century Kabbalist.

Twenty-five years later, in 5714 (1954), Rabbi Menachem M. Schneerson, who had succeeded his father-in-law as the Lubavitcher Rebbe in 5710 (1950), taught an exposition on that discourse. In 5739 (1978), to commemorate the Rebbe and Rebbetzin's fiftieth wedding anniversary, this exposition was reviewed and edited by the Rebbe and published as an official discourse.

THE DISCOURSE OF 5689

In *Lecha Dodi, 5689*, Rabbi Yosef Yitzchak describes the custom at the *Kabbalat Panim*:

"In the order of the wedding ceremony, first the guests come to welcome the groom. Then, they walk together with the groom to 'welcome the bride,' at which point the groom covers the bride's face with the veil. Finally, they proceed to the *chuppah*."

GIVER AND RECEIVER

"The deeper meaning of this is: In order for there to be any union of giver and receiver, the receiver must 'ascend,' so as to draw close to the giver. But before this can occur, the giver must first establish an external connection with the receiver, by giving something of his external faculties that will touch the external faculties of the receiver. This in turn enables the receiver to lift himself up, to rise until he becomes close to the standing of the giver, so that he may then receive from the giver the deeper, internal transmission."

TWO EXAMPLES

To explain this, Rabbi Yosef Yitzchak gave two examples of "giver/receiver" relationships where this idea plays out: teacher and student, and father and son.

The first example: When the Talmudic sage Rabbah would begin teaching his students, he would make a humorous remark before beginning his lesson. Literally, the Talmud's expression is: "Before Rabbah would open *[to] his students*...." Chasidus explains that this unusual expression alludes to the fact that before a teacher can impart of his wisdom, he must first "open" the faculties of his students, so that they will be ready to receive his teachings. Rabbah accomplished this by making a humorous remark before he began teaching.

The humorous remark was only a starting point and merely established a basic, "external" connection between Rabbah and his students. The ultimate purpose, however, was to forge a deeper, more "internal" connection between the wisdom of Rabbah and the minds of his students, i.e., that they understand and grasp the lesson.

The second example: A father wishes to play with his very young son face to face. Since the child is small, the father must lower his hands until they are underneath the child, and then he must pick up the child until their faces are at the same level. Only then can the father speak with his child and play with him face to face.

In this example, the "internal transmission" is the father actually playing together with his son, as this is what makes the child happy. The act of picking up the child is (relative to their playing together) merely an "external" act for both father and child. For the father, picking up his son is a very limited interaction, one that does not openly express his love for his child (as playing together does). For the child, he does not (necessarily) sense his father's love in the act of picking up; the child merely sees that he is being brought closer to father (and may not even realize that it is his father who is lifting him). It is only later, when they actually play together, that the child feels the father's love.

PRAYER

This model—that basic, external connections engender deeper, internal ones—helps explain   the function of prayer in one's daily service of G-d: "Prayer is connection: through prayer one connects with G-d…and through prayer one transforms physical objects into conduits for G-dliness."

It is through prayer that one receives the power to transform all of one's physical affairs into conduits for G-dliness, allowing one to serve G-d even with physical matters. Prayer connects one with G-dliness, opening the coarse physical body to the radiance of one's soul. When this happens, all of one's mundane actions become permeated with a holy purpose. One will eat and drink not to satisfy the body's base cravings, but rather to energize one's self for studying Torah and fulfilling *mitzvot*; one will become involved in business matters not for greedy purposes, but rather in order to be able to assist those who are less fortunate.

The ability to transform physical matters into conduits for G-dliness represents Israel's "internal connection" with

G-d. However, there must first be a more general, external connection before the internal one can be made. This is why our Sages say that "only with a sense of earnestness may one begin to pray"[1]—which *Rashi* explains as referring to the quality of surrender and humility[2]—for humility establishes an initial, general connection between one and the Creator.

GROOM AND BRIDE

Accordingly, we can apply this reasoning to understand the *Kabbalat Panim* custom:

The purpose of the marriage is ultimately to procreate and produce offspring, which requires an internal union and transmission to bring to bear. However, before that can take place, there must first be an external union and transmission: the groom walking to welcome the bride and covering her face with a veil.

Hence we say *Come...to meet the bride*: It is an expression of the giver drawing close to the receiver to create an external connection, preparing the receiver for the deeper, internal transmission. This special relationship then elicits G-d's infinite power: granting offspring that are upright and blessed, children and grandchildren who are occupied with Torah and *mitzvot*.

THE DISCOURSE OF 5714

As mentioned earlier, the Rebbe expounded on the above in 5714 (1954), further developing some of the concepts of the discourse and relating them to the Kabbalistic counterparts of the groom and bride.

From the verse, *Let us make man in Our image, after Our likeness*,[3] we learn that physical man is created in the image and likeness of Supernal Man, a term which refers to the supernal *sefirot, or attributes*, of G-d. A groom and bride in par-

---

1. *Berachot* 5:1.

2. See *Rashi* to *Berachot* 30b, s.v. *koved rosh*. I.e., before a person begins praying to G-d he must surrender his

ego, and be humbled before Whom he stands.

3. Genesis 1:26. See *Shaloh*, Introduction (9b, 10a).

ticular correspond to the spiritual levels of *z'eyr anpin*[4] and *malchut*:[5] groom is *z'a*, and bride is *malchut*.

The relationship between *z'a* and *malchut* parallels the (physical, intimate) relationship between a physical groom and bride, where the groom (male) is the transmitter and the bride (female) is the recipient.

Now, the initial transmission from *z'a* to *malchut* can only be "external," i.e., from the exterior of *z'a* to the exterior of *malchut*, since the internal aspects of the former begin on a level higher than those of the latter. It does pave the way, however, for a transmission from the interior of *z'a* into the interior of *malchut*. Furthermore, the purpose of this internal transmission is to activate the root (*keter*) of *malchut*, which has a power greater than *z'a* itself. Subsequently, *malchut* (the recipient) will give to *z'a* (the giver), and raise *z'a* "ever higher" to a realm unattainable on its own.

Thus, this process has three primary points: 1) the external transmission from giver to receiver, which equips the receiver to receive 2) the subsequent internal union, which in turn causes 3) the activation of a latent power within the receiver that surpasses the level of the giver itself.

THE EXAMPLES

The discourse then revisits the examples cited in the first discourse, explaining how each demonstrates these ideas, along with additional applications to the concept of Shabbat and the relationship between groom and bride.

In the teacher/student relationship, there is an initial, external transmission from teacher to student: the humorous remark. This paves the way for the subsequent internal transmission: the actual lesson. But by teaching the students, the teacher rises "ever higher" in knowledge, as the sage who said,

---

4. Z'EYR ANPIN. Lit., "small face," this is the Kabbalistic term used collectively for the six *middot* or *sefirot* of *chesed, gevurah, tiferet, netzach, hod* and *yesod*. It is often abbreviated as *z'a*.

5. MALCHUT. Literally, Royalty or Kingship; the tenth and last of the *sefirot*. See further, below, notes at the beginning of *Lecha Dodi 5714*.

"From my students I learned more than from all the others"—a blessing unattainable without teaching.[6]

In the father/son relationship, the initial, external transmission from father to son is when the father picks up his son. This allows for the subsequent internal transmission as the father plays with the child. And this transmission elicits to the son the essence of the father, i.e., his inner, deep love for his son.

DAILY SERVICE AND PRAYER

In one's daily service of G-d, the three stages of external, internal, and essence are also present: The first statement in the morning, the Modeh Ani, establishes an external connection between a person and G-d. This then paves the way for a deeper, internal connection during prayer. Finally, by drawing G-d into all one's physical matters to the extent of transforming them into conduits of G-dliness, one provides an extra boost of strength to the G-dly soul, enabling it to reach "ever higher" than before, as Chasidus[7] interprets the verse, *Many crops come through the strength of an ox:*[8] Man possesses an animal soul in order to harness its coarse power for holy purposes by transforming all of one's physical affairs into conduits for G-dliness. One's G-dly soul cannot achieve this incredible, transformative act alone, and must first activate and concentrate the animal soul's power.

---

6. *Taanit* 7a, where the Talmud states, "R. Chanina said, 'I have learned much from my teachers. I learned more from my friends than from my teachers. But from my students I learned more than from all the others.'"

Chasidus explains that a teacher derives immense pleasure from teaching, for "absolute pleasure in having transmitted a lesson is possible only when the teacher sees that the student properly grasped the subject matter...for that is the purpose of his

teaching" (*B'Shaah Shehikdimu 5672*, vol. 2, p. 1120. See also *Torat Chaim, Vayigash* 89d ff). This implies that the student's grasping of the transmission is more valuable to the teacher than the actual transmission, and therefore, affects the teacher in a much more profound way.

7. See *Likkutei Torah, Haazinu* 75b, et al.

8. Proverbs 14:4.

SHABBAT

Shabbat, too, behaves both as a giver and receiver. On one hand, Shabbat "receives" from the days of the week, much like malchut receiving from z'a. In fact, z'a, the six *middot, correspond to the six weekdays, while malchut* corresponds to Shabbat. *Malchut* is the level through which the material world is created, and a person's task during the week is to work with the material world and refine the divine sparks trapped within it. On Shabbat, however, one "reaps the benefits" of this work, by enjoying the delight and pleasure generated from the week's work, when *malchut* returns to its source, taking along the refined divine sparks to a greater spiritual level.

Hence, our Sages say, "One who toils on Erev Shabbat will [have what to] eat on Shabbat."[9] Kabbalistically, this refers to the spiritual "food," or gain, brought about by refining physicality during the week, which are "given" to Shabbat to be enjoyed.

On the other hand, the *Zohar* tells us that "all the days [of the subsequent week] are blessed from Shabbat."[10] I.e., after *malchut* is elevated by (and through) the toil of the past week, it rises higher than z'a and actually transmits blessings into the following six weekdays. Thus, Shabbat becomes a "giver" to the subsequent week, blessing it to be greater than the previous week.

GROOM AND BRIDE

Finally, the discourse states, so it is with every giver and receiver: the giver actually gains through having given to the receiver. In the case of a groom and bride, the role of the groom is to reveal the bride's ability to procreate, an act impossible for the groom himself. Having made an internal transmission to the bride, the groom subsequently receives and gains from the bride, who can now express her "essential" power to elicit G-d's infinite power of creation, giving birth to offspring who are upright and blessed, children and grandchildren who are occupied with Torah and *mitzvot.*

---

9. *Avodah Zara* 3a.   10. See *Zohar* II:63b; 88a.

NOTE ON THE HEBREW TEXT: In vowelizing the Hebrew words in this edition we have followed the grammatical rules of the Holy Tongue, which occasionally differ from the traditional or colloquial pronunciation. The original footnotes to the Hebrew text were written by the Lubavitcher Rebbe, Rabbi Menachem M. Schneerson, and appear at the end of the *maamar*. Translation of these notes appears as footnotes to the main text, in bold type.

TRANSLATION
AND
COMMENTARY

With the Help of Heaven

Come, my Beloved, to meet the bride; let us welcome the Shabbat.[1]

Shabbat is called "bride" [as in the above-quoted passage]. Shabbat is also called "queen," as in the saying "the Shabbat queen."[2]

[The relationship between Shabbat and bride is underscored by the fact that] in the case of a physical groom and bride, the groom is called "king"—as it is stated in *Pirkei d'Rabbi Eliezer*, Ch. 16: "A groom is likened to a king"—and the bride is called "queen."[3]

SUPERNAL QUEEN

[To explain the concept of "queen":]

It is written, *Let us make man in Our image, after Our likeness.*[4] This means that physical man is [created] in the image and likeness of Supernal Man,[5] which refers to the supernal *sefirot.*[6]

---

1. This is the opening line of the *Lecha Dodi* hymn, composed by Rabbi Shlomo HaLevi Alkabetz, 16th-century Kabbalist, and sung every Friday night in the *Kabbalat Shabbat* service.

The commentaries explain that this passage is the Jewish people's invitation to G-d (*my Beloved*) to join in ushering in the Shabbat (*bride*).

2. See *Shabbat* 119a (cited below): "R. Chanina would wrap himself [in fine garments] and say, 'Come, let us go out and greet the Shabbat queen.' R. Yannai would don his [Shabbat] garment and say, 'Enter, O bride! Enter, O bride!'"

3. Both Shabbat and a bride are referred to by our Sages with the appellation "queen." This indicates that (in a deeper sense) there is a correlation between the concepts of Shabbat and a bride, the details of which will form the main discussion of this discourse.

4. Genesis 1:26. See *Shaloh*, Introduction (9b, 10a).

5. *Adam Ha'elyon*, in the Hebrew.

In his vision of the Divine Chariot, the prophet Ezekiel describes G-d appearing as *a man* (Ezekiel 1:26: *And upon the likeness of the throne there was a likeness like the appearance of a man upon it, from above*). This dimension of G-dliness is what the Kabbalists refer to as Supernal Man.

בס"ד

לְכָהֿ* דוֹדִי לִקְרַאת כַּלָּה פְּנֵי שַׁבָּת נְקַבְּלָהֿ,

וְהִנֵּה הַשַּׁבָּת נִקְרֵאת כַּלָּה וְנִקְרֵאת מַלְכָּה וְכַמַּאֲמָר שַׁבָּת מַלְכְּתָאֿ,

דְּהִנֵּה חָתָן וְכַלָּה הֲרֵי הֶחָתָן נִקְרָא מֶלֶךְ כְּדְאִיתָא בְּפִרְקֵי דְרַבִּי אֱלִיעֶזֶר פֶּרֶק ט"ז חָתָן דּוֹמֶה לְמֶלֶךְ וְהַכַּלָּה נִקְרֵאת מַלְכָּה,

דְּהִנֵּה כְּתִיבֿ נַעֲשֶׂהֿ אָדָם בְּצַלְמֵנוּ כִּדְמוּתֵנוּ דְּהָאָדָם שֶׁלְּמַטָּה הוּא בְּצֶלֶם וּדְמוּת אָדָם הָעֶלְיוֹן שֶׁהֵם הַסְּפִירוֹת הָעֶלְיוֹנוֹת,

Kabbalah and Chasidus thus explain the verse, *Let us make man in Our image, after Our likeness*, as meaning that terrestrial man is created in the image of Supernal Man.

Specifically, Supernal Man refers to the ten supernal *sefirot*, the ten Divine "powers" (attributes) G-d employs in creating and sustaining the world (see following note and reference cited there). Man is created in the image of Supernal Man, then, in the sense that man's soul, too, possesses these ten powers. See *Tanya*, Ch. 3, beg.

6. SEFIROT. In the introduction to *Tikkunei Zohar*, Elijah is quoted as saying: "You are He who has brought forth ten 'garments,' and we call them ten *sefirot*, through which to direct hidden worlds which are not revealed and revealed worlds."

There are ten creative Divine attributes and manifestations of G-d, called *sefirot*. These are: *chochmah*, *binah*, *daat*, *chesed*, *gevurah*, *tiferet*, *netzach*, *hod*, *yesod* and *malchut*. The *sefirot* are divided into two categories: the first three are *sechel* (intellectual attributes), the latter seven *middot* (emotive attributes). The ten *sefirot* manifest themselves in each of the four spiritual worlds of *Atzilut*, *Beriah*, *Yetzirah* and *Asiyah*, and are the source of (and parallel to) the ten powers of the human soul. Just as man reveals himself through his attributes, or their "garments" (thought, speech and deed), similarly G-d reveals Himself through His attributes, the *sefirot*. See Jacob Immanuel Schochet, *Mystical Concepts in Chassidism*, Ch. 3 (Kehot, 1988).

[Within the supernal *sefirot*], *z'eyr anpin*[7] of *Atzilut*[8] is called "king"[9]

—indeed, the statement that "the image of every soul stood before the Holy King"[10] is explained to be referring to *z'eyr anpin* of *Atzilut*[11]—

and the *sefirah* of *malchut*[12] is called "queen."[13]

Now, the *Zohar* states that "a king without a queen is neither a king nor great,"[14] since it is of primary importance for there to be a *union* of *z'a* and *malchut*.[15]

---

7. Z'EYR ANPIN. Literally "small face," this is the Kabbalistic term used collectively for the six *middot* or *sefirot* of *chesed, gevurah, tiferet, netzach, hod,* and *yesod*. It is often abbreviated as *z'a*.

8. ATZILUT. Kabbalah and Chasidus speak of four supernal worlds. Of these, *Atzilut* is the loftiest. It is a G-dly world (*Tanya*, Ch. 49). In *Atzilut*, there is no feeling of self or being, just an awareness of something higher, something beyond—G-dliness. *Atzilut* is therefore not considered to be a *created* world, but rather an *emanated* world. It is in *Atzilut* that G-d's attributes (the ten *sefirot*) are first manifest. For more on *Atzilut*, see *Mystical Concepts in Chassidism*, Ch. 4, and *The Four Worlds* (Kehot, 2003), pp. 24-28.

9. Since physical man is created in the "image" of the *sefirot*, it follows that the physical concept of king and queen has a spiritual counterpart—a concept of "king" and "queen" within the *sefirot*. The discourse now relates this idea.

To explain: Every soul consists of two parts, masculine and feminine. Born from a union between *z'a* and

malchut of *Atzilut*, the soul's masculine part—the "active transmitter" of divine light—has its source in *z'a*, while the feminine part—the "passive recipient"—has its source in *malchut*. "Masculine" and "feminine" also refer to "root" and revelation": the soul's root is in *z'a*, and its revelation in *malchut*. The male aspect, *z'a*, is called "king," while the female aspect, *malchut*, is called "queen." Hence the following quote in the main text, "every soul ... [with] the Holy King," namely, *z'a*, indicative of the masculine part of every soul (*Yom Tov Shel Rosh Hashanah 5666*, cited below, note 11).

10. In Chasidic literature, this phrase is attributed to the *Zohar*, though in our editions of *Zohar* this particular wording is not found. See *Zohar* I:90b, 227b, 333b; *Zohar* II:96b; *Zohar* III:61b, 104b.

11. See *Sefer Hamaamarim 5650*, p. 358; *Sefer Hamaamarim 5657*, p. 177; *Yom Tov Shel Rosh Hashanah 5666*, new edition, p. 207.

12. MALCHUT. Literally, royalty or kingship; the tenth and last of the *sefirot*. *Malchut* is referred to in the *Tik-*

דְּזָ"א [זְעֵיר אַנְפִּין] דַּאֲצִילוּת נִקְרָא מַלְכָּא

– וְכַמְבוֹאָרֹ בְּעִנְיָן דְּכָל נִשְׁמָתָא וְנִשְׁמָתָא הֲוָה קַיְּימָא
בְּדִיּוּקְנָאָה קַמֵּיהּ מַלְכָּא קַדִּישָׁאֹ שֶׁהוּא זָ"א דַּאֲצִילוּת –

וּסְפִירַת הַמַּלְכוּת נִקְרֵאת מַלְכְּתָא,

וְאִיתָא בְּזֹהַרֹ דְּמַלְכָּא בְּלָא מַטְרוּנִיתָא לַאו אִיהוּ מֶלֶךְ וְלַאו
אִיהוּ גָדוֹל, דְּהָעִיקָר הוּא יְחוּד זוּ"ן.

---

kunei Zohar (intro. 17a) as the
"Mouth of G-d," the Word or Speech
of G-d by which the world comes
into actual being. (Both mouth and
speech are used for communication
with "others" outside of self.) The
world and the created beings (the
"others") make it possible for there to
be a divine kingdom, since "there
cannot be a king without a nation,"
i.e., G-d cannot be a ruler without
the existence of the element of "other."

Eitz Chaim (6:5, 8:5, et passim)
speaks of malchut as being "a dim
speculum, because it has no (light) of
its own." The Zohar (I:249b, 251b)
therefore compares malchut to "the
moon that has no light of its own
save that which is given to it from the
sun." Paradoxically, although malchut
is a passive sefirah that only contains
that which the other sefirot pour into
it, it is specifically through malchut
that the original creative plan is actualized.

13. To continue from footnote
9—the relationship between z'a and
malchut parallels the (physical, intimate) relationship between a human
king and queen, in which the king
(male) is the transmitter and the
queen (female) is the recipient.

And when we say that "Shabbat"
and "bride" are called "queen," in a
deeper sense it means that they are
likened to the Supernal Queen—i.e.,
malchut of Atzilut.

14. Zohar III:5a. See also Zohar
I:256a; Zohar III:69a; Eichah Rabbah
5:19.

15. It would seem that in this z'a/
malchut (male/female) relationship,
z'a is of a higher stature, being that it
is the transmitter of G-dly light, while
malchut, being the recipient of this
light, is of a lower stature. Yet, the
Zohar states that without malchut, z'a
"is neither a king nor great." This is
because the purpose of z'a transmitting G-dly light is that it be received and contained within malchut;
if that does not occur, z'a has not realized its purpose.

Furthermore, the greatness of malchut is not limited to the fact that it
enables z'a to fulfill its purpose (of
transmitting G-dly light); for as the
discourse will now explain, malchut
ultimately serves as the catalyst for
eliciting an even greater G-dly
light—one that far surpasses the light
originally transmitted by z'a.

Likewise, [in the Torah's account of the creation of man
and woman] it is only after *male and female He created them*
that *G-d blessed them....*[16]

[So the female aspect (*malchut*) is the source of this blessing. And the same is true of "Shabbat" and "bride," who are
likened to "*malchut*/queen"—they too are sources of supernal
blessings.]

Therefore, just as Shabbat must be received with joy, as
Shabbat is the source of all supernal and terrestrial blessings,
and "all the days [of the subsequent week] are blessed from
Shabbat,"[17] similarly must the bride be received [with joy], as
she is the source of the lofty blessings.[18]

SAGES' PRECEDENT

Now,[19] the phrase, *Come, my Beloved, to meet the bride; let us
welcome the Shabbat* that is recited in the *Kabbalat Shabbat*
service is based on the following Talmudic passage (*Shabbat*
119a): As sunset on Friday evening came, R. Chanina would
wrap himself (in fine garments—*Rashi*) and stand and say,
"Come, let us go out and greet the Shabbat queen." R. Yannai would don his (Shabbat) garments on the eve of Shabbat
and say, "Enter, O bride! Enter, O bride!" (this was a term of
endearment—*Rashi*).

Likewise, *Zohar* II:272b states: All forms of Shabbat preparation should be made before Shabbat, whether it be preparing the food, drink, clothing or lounge. One should prepare a fine recliner with many pillows and embroidered covers
from the best of all that is found in the house, just as one prepares a marriage chamber for a bride—for Shabbat is a
"queen" and a "bride."

For just as Shabbat is the source of the blessings, likewise
is rejoicing with the groom and bride and receiving them
[with joy] the source of the blessings.

---

16. Genesis 1:27-28. Man alone was
unworthy of G-d's blessing; it was
only after G-d created the woman
that He blessed them both, and said

to them, *Be fruitful and multiply....*
The reason for this is because, as
mentioned above, the "transmitter"
(man) cannot realize his purpose (*Be*

וּכְתִיב[יח] זָכָר וּנְקֵבָה בָּרָא אֹתָם, וַיְבָרֶךְ אֹתָם אֱלֹקִים כו׳,

וְלָזֹאת הִנֵּה כְּדוּגְמַת הַשַּׁבָּת שֶׁצְּרִיכִים לְקַבְּלוֹ בְּשִׂמְחָה דְּשַׁבָּת אִיהִי מְקוֹרָא דְּכָל בִּרְכָאן עִילָּאִין וְתַתָּאִין, דְּכוּלְּהוּ יוֹמִין מִתְבָּרְכִין מֵהַשַּׁבָּת[יט], הִנֵּה כְּמוֹ כֵן צְרִיכִים לְקַבֵּל פְּנֵי כַּלָּה דְּאִיהִי מְקוֹרָא דְּבִרְכָתָא עִילָּאָה.

וְהִנֵּה[יט] יְסוֹד מַאֲמָר זֶה דְּלְכָה דוֹדִי לִקְרַאת כַּלָּה פְּנֵי שַׁבָּת נְקַבְּלָה שֶׁאוֹמְרִים בְּקַבָּלַת הַשַּׁבָּת הוּא דְּאִיתָא בִּגְמָרָא (שַׁבָּת קי״ט עַמּוּד א׳) רַבִּי חֲנִינָא מִיעֲטַּף (בִּבְגָדִים נָאִים, רַשִׁ״י) וְקָאֵי אַפַּנְיָא דְּמַעֲלֵי שַׁבַּתָּא אָמַר בּוֹאוּ וְנֵצֵא לִקְרַאת שַׁבָּת הַמַּלְכָּה, רַבִּי יַנַּאי לָבֵישׁ מָאנֵיהּ (בִּגְדֵי שַׁבָּת) מַעֲלֵי שַׁבָּת וְאָמַר בּוֹאִי כַלָּה בּוֹאִי כַלָּה (הָכִי קָרֵי לָהּ לִשְׁבִיתַת שַׁבָּת מִתּוֹךְ חֲבִיבוּת, רַשִׁ״י),

וּבַזֹּהַר חֵלֶק ג׳ דַּף רע״ב עַמּוּד ב׳ אִיתָא וּבְשַׁבָּת בְּכָל מִלּוֹי צָרִיךְ לְאִתּוֹסָפָא מֵחוֹל עַל הַקֹּדֶשׁ בֵּין בְּמַאֲכָלָיו וּבְמִשְׁתָּיו[כ], בֵּין בִּלְבוּשֵׁיהּ, בֵּין בַּהֲסִבָּתֵיהּ דְּצָרִיךְ לְתַקָּנָא לֵיהּ מְסִבָּה שַׁפִּירָא בְּכַמָּה כָּרִים וּכְסָתוֹת מְרַקְּמָן מִכָּל דְּאִית בְּבֵיתֵיהּ כְּמַאן דְּתָקִין חוּפָּה לְכַלָּה, דְּשַׁבַּתָּא אִיהִי מַלְכְּתָא וְאִיהִי כַּלָּה.

וְהַיְינוּ דְּכְשֵׁם שֶׁהַשַּׁבָּת הִיא מְקוֹר הַבְּרָכוֹת הִנֵּה כְּמוֹ כֵן שִׂמְחַת חָתָן וְכַלָּה וְקַבָּלַת פְּנֵיהֶם הִיא מְקוֹר הַבְּרָכוֹת.

---

fruitful and multiply...) without a "recipient" (woman).

17. *Zohar* II:63b; 88a.

18. This equivalency is reflected in
the *Lecha Dodi* hymn, which equates

welcoming a bride with welcoming
the Shabbat.

19. The discourse now cites sayings of
our Sages which express the equivalency between Shabbat and bride.

ENCOMPASSING CHUPPAH

It[20] is written, *For over all the honor there will be a chuppah* (canopy).[21] [The word *all* indicates that] there are two kinds of "honor" [encompassed by this *chuppah*]: the honor of the groom, and the honor of the bride.[22]

[In the context of G-d's relationship with the Jewish people] G-d is called the "groom," and the Jewish people are called His "bride," as the Sages comment [on the scriptural phrase], *On His wedding day*[23]—"this is the Giving of the Torah."[24]

And "honor" refers to a quality that "encompasses."[25] [Thus,] the "honor of the groom" refers to G-d's love of the Jewish people,[26] as it is written, *"I have loved you," says G-d.*[27] The "honor of the bride" is the Jewish people's love of G-d, as it is written, *My soul yearns, indeed it pines [for the courtyards of the Lord].*[28]

And the "*chuppah*" [is an even loftier level that] generally encompasses both "groom" and "bride."[29]

---

20. At this point the discourse proceeds by discussing the deeper meaning of the *chuppah* and the "welcoming of the bride."

21. Isaiah 4:5. This verse in Isaiah's prophecy of the Messianic era speaks of the divine protection that will be afforded to the righteous, to protect them from the destruction that will rain down upon the wicked: *When the L-rd will have washed the filth of the daughters of Zion and rinsed the blood of Jerusalem from her midst, with a spirit of judgment and a spirit of purging. G-d will create over every structure of Mount Zion and over those who assemble in it a cloud by day, and smoke and a glow of flaming fire by night, for over all the honor there will be a* chuppah (ibid., 4-5).

Chasidus explains that there is great significance in Isaiah's use of the word *chuppah* to describe G-d's protective presence over the Jewish people—"protecting the Jewish people's honor." It indicates an aspect of G-d's presence that "covers" and unites G-d and the Jewish people, much like a wedding *chuppah* that unites groom and bride (*Likkutei Torah, Shir Hashirim,* 47b ff.; *Siddur im Dach,* 28d ff.; *Maamarei Admur Ha'emtzaei, Derushei Chatunah,* p. 1 ff.; ibid., p. 7).

22. The verse's inclusion of the seemingly superfluous word "*all*" alludes to the fact that this *chuppah* "covers" more than one type of "honor"—the honor of the groom and the honor of the bride.

23. Song of Songs 3:11.

דְּהִנֵּה כְּתִיב²⁴ כִּי עַל כָּל כָּבוֹד חֻפָּה שֶׁהֵם ב' בְּחִינוֹת
כְּבוֹד חָתָן וּכְבוֹד כַּלָּה,

דְּחָתָן הוּא הַקָּדוֹשׁ בָּרוּךְ הוּא וְכַמַּאֲמָרִ²י בְּיוֹם חֲתוּנָתוֹ
זוֹ מַתַּן תּוֹרָה שֶׁהַקָּדוֹשׁ בָּרוּךְ הוּא נִקְרָא חָתָן וּכְנֶסֶת
יִשְׂרָאֵל נִקְרֵאת כַּלָּה,

וְכָבוֹד הוּא בְּחִינַת מַקִּיף, כְּבוֹד חָתָן אַהֲבַת הַקָּדוֹשׁ
בָּרוּךְ הוּא לִכְנֶסֶת יִשְׂרָאֵל כְּמוֹ שֶׁכָּתוּב²י אָהַבְתִּי אֶתְכֶם אָמַר
הוי', וּכְבוֹד כַּלָּה אַהֲבַת כְּנֶסֶת יִשְׂרָאֵל לְהַקָּדוֹשׁ בָּרוּךְ הוּא
וּכְמוֹ שֶׁכָּתוּב²י נִכְסְפָה וְגַם כָּלְתָה נַפְשִׁי,

וְהַחֻפָּה הוּא הַמַּקִּיף הַכְּלָלִי עַל חָתָן וְכַלָּה.

---

24. See *Taanit* 26b. Just as a wedding
facilitates the union of a man and
woman, so did the Giving of the Torah facilitate a union between G-d and
the Jewish people. Within this union,
G-d is called the "groom," as He is the
Giver, and the Jewish people are called
the "bride," being the receiver.

25. I.e., as opposed to an aspect that
"permeates."

To explain: Some qualities are
more internal and others more external. Knowledge, for example, is an
internal quality. When one is given
knowledge it enters and is collected
within his mind. Honor, however, is
an external quality. The honor bestowed upon a person does not enter
within him, but "surrounds" him and
lifts him up to a higher stature.

26. In the groom/bride relationship,
it is their love for one another that encompasses, surrounds, and envelops
them: the bride is completely enveloped by her groom's love, and the

groom is completely enveloped by his
bride's love.

The same is true in the groom/
bride relationship between G-d and
the Jewish people: the Jewish people
are enveloped by G-d's love (the
"*honor* of the groom"), and G-d is enveloped by the Jewish people's love
(the "*honor* of the bride").

27. Malachi 1:2.

28. Psalms 84:2.

29. Both groom and bride possess aspects that are "encompassing"—their
love for one another. Yet, in order for
there to be the *union* of groom and
bride, who are two distinct (and even
opposing) entities, an even greater encompassing force—the *chuppah*—is
required. The *chuppah*, which surrounds both groom and bride, represents an encompassing G-dly light so
lofty that it is capable of joining these
two forces together.

[In a more mystical sense, the dif-

THE MARRIAGE CEREMONY

The same is true in the physical realm.[30] In the order of the wedding ceremony, first the guests come to welcome the groom. Then, they walk together with the groom to "welcome the bride," at which point the groom covers the bride's face with the veil. Finally, they proceed to the *chuppah*.

The deeper meaning of this is: In order for there to be any union of giver and receiver, the receiver must "ascend," so as to draw close to the giver. But before this can occur, the giver must first establish an external connection with the receiver by giving something of his external faculties that will touch the external faculties of the receiver. This in turn enables the receiver to lift himself up, to rise until he becomes close to the standing of the giver, so that he may then receive from the giver the deeper, internal transmission.[31]

Summary

The discourse explains that a groom and bride correspond [respectively] to the supernal *sefirot* of *z'a* and *malchut*; "welcoming the bride" is similar to "welcoming the Shabbat," which is the source of blessing for all the days of the week; the

---

ference between "groom" and "bride" is thus:

"Groom" refers to the G-dly light that descends from on high to draw near to the souls of the Jewish people. (The Hebrew word for groom, *chattan*, is related to the word *chot*, which means "descend" (see *Yevamot* 63a).) "Bride" refers to the raising up of the souls of the Jewish people to draw close to G-dliness. (The Hebrew word for bride, *kallah*, can be read as *kalah* ("expire"), which is used in Scripture to refer to an intense yearning for G-d, to the point where the soul nearly "expires" from its deep rapture—see Psalms ibid.) To bring these two (opposing) forces together,

there must be a *chuppah*—the revelation of a G-dly light so lofty that it can contain both "groom" and "bride" and unite them as one (*Likkutei Torah*, ibid.).]

In the context of the verse quoted at the beginning of this section, the *chuppah* represents the union of the Jewish people's (encompassing) love of G-d with G-d's (encompassing) love of them.

30. It has heretofore been explained that it is the "*chuppah*" that encompasses G-d and the Jewish people that allows there to be the union between them. The discourse now explains that the same concept applies

וְכֵן הוּא לְמַטָּה, דְּהַסֵּדֶר הוּא שֶׁבָּאִים רוֹב עָם לְקַבֵּל פְּנֵי
הֶחָתָן, וְאַחַר כַּךְ הוֹלְכִים עִם הֶחָתָן לְקַבֵּל פְּנֵי הַכַּלָּה, וְהֶחָתָן
מְכַסֶּה בְּצָעִיף אֶת הַכַּלָּה וְהוֹלְכִים אֶל הַחוּפָּה.

וְהָעִנְיָן הוּא[m] דְּבְכָל עֲלִיַּת הַמְקַבֵּל אֶל הַמַּשְׁפִּיעַ צָרִיךְ
לִהְיוֹת תְּחִלָּה הַמְשָׁכַת הַמַּשְׁפִּיעַ בִּבְחִינַת חִיצוֹנִיּוּת שֶׁבּוֹ
לִבְחִינַת חִיצוֹנִיּוּת הַמְקַבֵּל, כְּדֵי שֶׁעַל יְדֵי הַמְשָׁכָה זוֹ יוּכַל
הַמְקַבֵּל לִישָׂא אֶת עַצְמוֹ וּלְהִתְעַלּוֹת לִהְיוֹת קָרוֹב
לְמַדְרֵיגַת הַמַּשְׁפִּיעַ וְאָז יְקַבֵּל הַמְשָׁכָה הַפְּנִימִית מֵהַמַּשְׁפִּיעַ.

קיצוּר.

יְבָאֵר כִּי חָתָן וְכַלָּה הֵם בְּדוּגְמַת הַסְּפִירוֹת הָעֶלְיוֹנוֹת
ז״א וּמַלְכוּת, וְקַבָּלַת פְּנֵי הַכַּלָּה הוּא כְּדוּגְמַת קַבָּלַת פְּנֵי
הַשַּׁבָּת שֶׁהִיא הַבְּרָכָה לְכָל יְמֵי הַשָּׁבוּעַ, כְּבוֹד חָתָן אַהֲבַת

---

to a physical *chuppah*: it too allows for the union of groom and bride. But before the *chuppah* can occur, there must first be the ceremonial "welcoming of the bride," in which the groom covers the bride's face with the veil. The purpose of this ceremony in this context will now be explained.

31. To better clarify the concept being discussed, let us focus on one example of the "giver/receiver" relationship: the relationship between a mentor and his protégé. The mentor's goal is that he and his protégé will become so close that ultimately the protégé will begin to think and act as he does. The mentor wishes to share a deep, personal connection with his protégé. However, since the protégé is initially much lower than the mentor, the mentor must first raise the protégé to his (higher) level. Without doing this, the mentor's attempt to share with protégé cannot be received by the faculties of the protégé, let alone establish a deep connection.

Therefore, the mentor himself must raise the protégé by first establishing a very basic, "external" connection with the protégé, one which his faculties can receive and appreciate as the beginning of a relationship. This acts as a starting point for them to ultimately realize a deeper, more meaningful relationship.

This, then, is the deeper significance of the *kabbalat panim* ceremony: The groom (the "giver") approaches the bride (the "receiver") and covers her face with the veil, establishing a very basic, "external" connection. This raises the bride up to a higher standing, and enables the *chuppah*, when groom and bride unite in a deeper, more internal way.

"honor of the groom" refers to G-d's love for the Jewish people, and the "honor of the bride" refers to the Jewish people's love for G-d; the "*chuppah*" is the essential transmission; before the *chuppah*, the groom covers the bride's face with a veil, which is the connection between the external faculties of the giver with the external faculties of the receiver, so that there may be a deeper, more essential transmission and reception.

2.

The explanation of this is:[32]

Our Sages relate (*Pesachim* 117a): Before Rabbah[33] would open [to begin teaching] his students, he would make a humorous remark, which would cause his students to laugh. After that, he would sit in awe and open [to begin teaching] his teachings.[34]

The "giver" must "open his *students*,"[35] i.e., he must prepare the "receiver" to be fit to receive the transmission [of his teachings] by first exciting their senses and faculties. Then he must [make another preparation to] "open his *teachings*," which entails ensuring that his teachings are measured according to the faculties of the students.[36]

---

32. In this chapter, the discourse will further explain the concept mentioned at the end of Chapter 1—namely, that before there can be the deeper, more "internal" connection between giver and receiver, the giver must first establish a basic "external" connection with the receiver.

The discourse cites two examples of "giver/receiver" relationships where this idea plays out: in the relationship between teacher and student, and in the relationship between father and son. (As to the significance of these two examples, see *Lecha Dodi 5714*, Chapters 2 and 3.)

33. This version ("Rabbah") is found in the Talmud and *Ein Yaakov*. *Tanya*, Ch. 7, however, cites an alternative version found in *Rabbeinu Chananel*, and also in *Yalkut Shimoni, Remez* 227, that says "Rava." One could analyze *Dikdukei Sofrim* and *Shabbat* 30b (gloss of the Lubavitcher Rebbe, Rabbi Menachem M. Schneerson, on the discourse entitled *Semuchim La'ad, 5680*, by Rabbi Shalom DovBer of Lubavitch (*Sefer Hamaamarim 5680*, p. 149)).

34. Rabbah's method of teaching his students demonstrates the process required for there to be any trans-

הַקָּדוֹשׁ בָּרוּךְ הוּא לִכְנֶסֶת יִשְׂרָאֵל, וּכְבוֹד כַּלָּה אַהֲבַת כְּנֶסֶת יִשְׂרָאֵל לְהַקָּדוֹשׁ בָּרוּךְ הוּא, וְהַחוּפָּה הוּא הַמְשָׁכַת הָעַצְמוּת וְקוֹדֶם הַחוּפָּה הֶחָתָן מְכַסֶּה אֶת הַכַּלָּה בְּצָעִיף שֶׁהוּא קֵירוּב חִיצוֹנִיּוּת הַמַּשְׁפִּיעַ אֶל חִיצוֹנִיּוּת הַמְקַבֵּל בִּשְׁבִיל הַשְׁפָּעָה וְקַבָּלָה פְּנִימִיּוּת.

ב.

וּבֵיאוּר הָעִנְיָן הוּא,

דְּהִנֵּה אָמְרוּ רַזַ"ל [רַבּוֹתֵינוּ זִכְרוֹנָם לִבְרָכָה] (פְּסָחִים דַּף קִי"ז עַמּוּד א') רַבָּה מִקַּמֵּי דְּפָתַח לְהוּ לְרַבָּנָן אָמַר מִילְתָא דִּבְדִיחוּתָא וּבָדְחוּ רַבָּנָן וְלִבְסוֹף יָתִיב בְּאֵימְתָא וּפָתַח בִּשְׁמַעְתָּא,

דְּהַמַּשְׁפִּיעַ צָרִיךְ לִפְתוֹחַ לְהוּ לְרַבָּנָן וְהַיְינוּ לַעֲשׂוֹת אֶת הַמְקַבֵּל רָאוּי לְקַבֵּל דְּבַר הַהַשְׁפָּעָה עַל יְדֵי פְּתִיחַת הַכֵּלִים וְהַחוּשִׁים שֶׁלּוֹ וְצָרִיךְ לִפְתוֹחַ בִּשְׁמַעְתָּא שֶׁיִּהְיֶה דְּבַר הַהַשְׁפָּעָה לְפִי עֵרֶךְ הַמְקַבֵּל,

---

mission from "giver" to "receiver," as the discourse will now explain.

(See *Lecha Dodi 5714*, chapter 2: "The story about Rabbah is first employed as an analogy by Rabbi Dov-Ber, second Lubavitcher Rebbe, in *Torat Chaim*, discourse entitled *V'eleh Toldot*, Ch. 6 (2d)... not as an analogy for the concept of *Lecha Dodi*. In *Semuchim La'ad, 5680...* it says that "*perhaps*" there is a connection between the concept of Rabbah's humorous remark and that of *Lecha Dodi*. But in *Lecha Dodi 5689* my father-in-law, the Rebbe, omitted the word "perhaps" and wrote it as obvious." See further, ibid., for a discussion of the source of

this example being used as an analogy for the concept of *Lecha Dodi*.)

35. Literally, the Talmud's expression is: "Before Rabbah would *open his students*...." This unusual expression alludes to the fact that before a teacher can impart of his wisdom, he must first "open" the faculties of his students, so that they will be ready to receive his teachings. Rabbah accomplished this by making a humorous remark before he began teaching. See *Torat Chaim* and *Sefer Hamaamarim 5680*, ibid.

36. I.e., the teacher must make cer-

Therefore, before he "opened his students," to prepare them to be ready to receive his teachings, Rabbah would make a humorous remark.

INCONSPICUOUS WISDOM

Now, this humorous remark can be categorized as "casual conversation," of which it says that even "the 'casual conversation' of Torah sages must be learned and studied,"[37] since these sayings contain great wisdom and intellectual depth.[38] Nonetheless, these sayings are considered to be merely an external representation of the sage.[39]

The greater the sage, the greater his "casual conversation" will be, from which many lofty concepts can be learned.[40] And although these sayings represent just the "fallen"[41] wisdom of the sage, they are still actual wisdom [that contain much depth]—as our Sages say (*Ketubot* 103a), "The statements of the Sages are blessings, the statements of the Sages are wealth, the statements of the Sages heal."[42]

This is referred to as "attending to a Torah scholar."[43] The

---

tain that his lesson is not too advanced for his students, one that they can fully understand and grasp with their minds.

Thus, there are two steps a teacher must take if he wants to ensure that his teachings will be understood by his students: 1) he must first prepare his *students* for receiving the lesson, which can be accomplished by engaging his students' minds with a humorous remark; 2) he must also prepare *himself* to give the lesson, by reviewing the lesson in his own mind to insure that it will be understandable to his students (and not above them).

37. *Sukkah* 21b; *Avodah Zarah* 19b. See *Rashi* on *Sukkah*, ibid.: "One must listen attentively even to the casual conversation of the Sages, for

from these words Torah thoughts can be derived…. One must listen to them and take them to heart." *Rashi* on *Avodah Zarah*, ibid., comments: "One ought to [even] listen to the casual conversation of the Sages so that he may learn how to speak in the *manner* of the Sages, whose words are pure, rich, and offer healing." See following footnote.

38. Rabbah, the great Talmudic sage, did not engage in mere frivolity. Even those remarks that the Talmud refers to as "humorous" were sayings (albeit "casual" ones) uttered by a Torah sage, and, as such, contained much wisdom and depth. They are sayings that one can—and therefore must—learn from.

39. Although there is much to be learned from even the casual con-

וְלָזֹאת הִנֵּה מִיקַמֵּי דְּפָתַח לְהוּ לְרַבָּנָן לַעֲשׂוֹתָם לִכְלֵי
קַבָּלָה אָמַר מִילְתָא דִּבְדִיחוּתָא,

וּמִילְתָא דִּבְדִיחוּתָא הוּא שִׂיחַת חוּלִין, וְעִם הֱיוֹת
דְּשִׂיחוֹת חוּלִין שֶׁל תַּלְמִידֵי חֲכָמִים צְרִיכִים לִימּוּד[ל], לְפִי
שֶׁיֵּשׁ בָּהֶם חָכְמָה רַבָּה וּשְׂכָלִים עֲמוּקִים, וּמִכָּל מָקוֹם הוּא
בְּחִינַת חִיצוֹנִיּוּת.

וַהֲגַם דְּמִי שֶׁהוּא גָּדוֹל יוֹתֵר הֲרֵי גַּם הַשִּׂיחוֹת חוּלִין
שֶׁלּוֹ הֵם בְּמַדְרֵיגָה גָּבוֹהַּ יוֹתֵר שֶׁיֵּשׁ לִלְמוֹד מֵהֶם הַרְבֵּה
עִנְיָנִים נִפְלָאִים, וְעִם כִּי זֶהוּ רַק נוֹבְלוֹת בִּלְבָד וּמִכָּל מָקוֹם הֵן
הֵן גּוּפֵי חָכְמָה וּכְמַאֲמַר רַזַ"ל (כְּתוּבּוֹת ק"ג עַמּוּד א') לְשׁוֹן
חֲכָמִים בִּרְכָה, לְשׁוֹן חֲכָמִים עוֹשֶׁר, לְשׁוֹן חֲכָמִים מַרְפֵּא,

וְהוּא שְׁמוּשָׁהּ שֶׁל תּוֹרָה, וְאָמְרוּ רַזַ"ל (בְּרָכוֹת דַּף ז'

---

versation of Torah sages, these sayings in no way represent the true depth and brilliance of the sage.

In Chasidus, the deep, brilliant thoughts of the Torah sage are referred to as his "inner" dimension (*penimiyut*), as they reflect his true and inner brilliance. His humorous remarks (and casual conversation), conversely, are referred to as merely his "external" dimension (*chitzoniyut*), as they do not capture his true and inner brilliance.

40. I.e., the sage's greatness is reflected (also) in his casual conversation, as his casual conversation is commensurate to his brilliance.

41. NOVLOT, in the Hebrew. *Novlot* refers to something "fallen," like the fallen leaves of a tree. The casual conversation of a Torah sage obviously does not contain his deepest, most

brilliant thoughts, but rather his "fallen" wisdom, those thoughts that have "descended" and pertain to more mundane matters. Nonetheless, as the discourse will say, even the sage's "fallen" wisdom is still *wisdom*—the wisdom of a true Torah sage—and is therefore rich with depth and meaning.

(A similar idea is expressed regarding Torah itself. *Bereishit Rabbah* 17:5 states: "Torah is 'fallen' supernal wisdom." Chasidus explains that this must be so because "Torah speaks [primarily] of *physical* matters" (*Torah Or, Lech Lecha* 11c).)

42. "Blessings, wealth and healing can be derived from the words of the Sages"—*Rashi* on *Ketubot* ad loc.

43. I.e., learning and studying the "casual" statements of Torah sages to discover the depth and wisdom they

Talmud states (*Berachot* 7b): "Attending to a Torah scholar is greater than studying under him, as it says, *Elisha son of Shaphat is here, who poured water over the hands of Elijah.*[44] The verse does not attribute Elisha's greatness to the fact that he studied under Elijah, but rather to his pouring water over Elijah's hands. This teaches us that attending to a Torah scholar is greater than studying under him."[45]

FORGING A CONNECTION

"After that, [Rabbah] would sit in awe and open [begin] his teachings." Torah must be studied amidst fear of heaven. Our Sages teach that just as the Jewish people received the Torah at Sinai with awe, fear, trembling and perspiration, so, too, must one feel whenever he studies Torah.[46] Just as Scripture states by the Giving of the Torah, *The people saw and trembled and stood from afar,*[47] similarly whenever one studies Torah it must be with great subordination and fear.

But before the Torah student can begin studying, the teacher must "open" his faculties. And this is accomplished by the teacher's humorous remark.

The humorous remark that precedes the lesson raises the students to a higher standing, so that they will be able to receive and understand the teacher's lesson.[48]

Now, in our scenario, the teacher is *incomparably* greater than the student.[49] It is for this reason that the student must be completely subordinated before his teacher, as our Sages

---

contain is what is meant by the Talmud phrase "*attending* to a Torah scholar." And this, the Talmud states, is greater than *studying* the scholar's actual Torah thoughts.

44. II Kings 3:11.

45. The discourse has thus described the greatness of the casual conversation of Torah sages, which is why Rabbah's humorous remark had the power to "open" the faculties of his students and prepare them to receive his teachings.

Nonetheless, the humorous remark is only a starting point, and merely establishes a basic "external" connection between a teacher and his students. The ultimate purpose is that the students understand and grasp the teacher's lesson, which forges a deeper, more "internal" connection between them, as the discourse will explain.

עַמּוּד ב') גְּדוֹלָה שִׁמּוּשָׁהּ שֶׁל תּוֹרָה יוֹתֵר מִלְּמוּדָהּ שֶׁנֶּאֱמַר‎[‎]
פֹּה אֱלִישָׁע בֶּן שָׁפָט אֲשֶׁר יָצַק מַיִם עַל יְדֵי אֵלִיָּהוּ, לָמַד לֹא
נֶאֱמַר אֶלָּא יָצַק מְלַמֵּד שֶׁגְּדוֹלָה שִׁמּוּשָׁהּ יוֹתֵר מִלְּמוּדָהּ.

וְהִנֵּה לְבַסּוֹף יָתִיב בְּאֵימְתָא וּפָתַח בִּשְׁמַעְתְּתָא, דְּלִימּוּד
הַתּוֹרָה צָרִיךְ לִהְיוֹת בְּיִרְאַת שָׁמַיִם, וְכַמַּאֲמָר‎[‎] מַה לְהַלָּן
בְּאֵימָה בְּיִרְאָה בְּרֶתֶת וּבְזֵיעָה אַף כָּאן כו', וְהַיְינוּ דִּכְשֵׁם
שֶׁבְּמַתַּן תּוֹרָה כְּתִיב‎[‎] וַיַּרְא הָעָם וַיָּנֻעוּ וַיַּעַמְדוּ מֵרָחוֹק
הִנֵּה כְּמוֹ כֵן בְּעֵת לִימּוּד הַתּוֹרָה צָרִיךְ לִהְיוֹת בְּבִיטּוּל
גָּדוֹל וּבְיִרְאָה גְּדוֹלָה,

אֲבָל קוֹדֶם צָרִיךְ הָרַב לִפְתּוֹחַ חוּשֵׁי הַמְקַבֵּל וְהוּא עַל
יְדֵי מִילְתָא דִּבְדִיחוּתָא.

וְיָדוּעַ‎[‎] דִּכְלָלוּת עִנְיַן הַבְּדִיחוּתָא שֶׁלִּפְנֵי הַלִּימּוּד הוּא
לְהַעֲלוֹת וּלְהַגְבִּיהַּ אֶת הַתַּלְמִידִים שֶׁיִּהְיוּ בְּעֵרֶךְ לְקַבֵּל אֶת
הַהַשְׁפָּעָה שֶׁיַּשְׁפִּיעַ לָהֶם הַמַּשְׁפִּיעַ.

דְּרַב וְתַלְמִיד אֵינָם בְּעֵרֶךְ זֶה לָזֶה, וְהַתַּלְמִיד צָרִיךְ לִהְיוֹת
בְּבִיטּוּל לִפְנֵי רַבּוֹ וְכַמַּאֲמָר‎[‎] כָּל תַּלְמִיד חָכָם הַיּוֹשֵׁב לִפְנֵי

---

46. *Berachot* 22a. See *Torah Or, Yitro* 67b.

47. Exodus 20:15.

48. As explained above, the teacher's humorous remark also contains wisdom, for it is the "casual conversation" of a Torah scholar. So when the teacher makes a humorous remark, his students have already received some of his wisdom. That in itself raises the students and prepares them for the lesson, when they will receive the deeper elements of his wisdom.

49. The reason why the teacher has to "raise" the student before he teaches him is because in this scenario the teacher is infinitely more brilliant and learned than the student. It would be impossible for the student, in his natural state, to be able to grasp the teacher's lesson. The teacher must therefore first draw the student somewhat closer to him—an act that is accomplished through making a humorous remark.

say, "A Torah scholar who sits before his teacher and whose lips do not drip with bitter dread...."[50] This refers to a state of complete subordination.[51]

This is the function of the humorous remark: to empower the student to be able to receive the words of the teacher. Generally speaking, it opens the heart and mind of the student, so that he will be a worthy recipient.[52]

Although the humorous remark merely creates an external connection between teacher and student,[53] nonetheless this external connection paves the way for their deeper, more internal connection; for it is specifically through the closeness initiated by the teacher telling [his students] a humorous remark that they can ultimately receive the "internal transmission" of his teachings.[54]

A FATHER'S LOVE

Take, for example,[55] a father who wishes to play with his very young son face-to-face. Since the child is small, the father must lower his hands—which are normally above the child's head—until they are underneath the child, and then he must pick up the child until the child is at the same level as his head. Only then can the father speak with his child and play with him face-to-face.

---

50. *Pesachim* 117a; *Shabbat* 30b. The full Talmudic quote reads: "A Torah scholar who sits before his teacher and whose lips do not drip with bitter dread is destined to be singed [in the fires of *Gehinnom*]."

51. Normally, one who is trying to understand his teacher's lesson would have to actively engage his mind while listening to the lesson. Here, however, where the teacher's brilliance is so great that the student is deemed "incomparable" to the teacher, the student cannot attempt to understand the lesson while the teacher is delivering it. Rather, he must sit with complete subordination, absorbing his master's words. Only later is he to review the lesson so as to understand it.

52. Since we are speaking of a student who is completely inferior to his teacher, the teacher must first engage him with a humorous remark; this raises the student to a higher level and opens his faculties (i.e., his heart and mind), as explained above.

53. As explained above, the brilliant sage's humorous remark is a most external representation of his genius. Furthermore, this remark does not

רַבּוֹ וְאֵין שְׂפְתוֹתָיו נוֹטְפוֹת מוֹר כו' שֶׁהוּא בְּתַכְלִית הַבִּטוּל,

וְלֹזֹאת הִנֵּה הַבְּדִיחוּתָא הוּא נוֹתֵן כֹּחַ בְּהַתַּלְמִיד שֶׁיּוּכַל לְקַבֵּל דִּבְרֵי רַבּוֹ, וּבְדֶרֶךְ כְּלָל הוּא פּוֹעֵל פְּתִיחַת הַלֵּב וְהַמּוֹחַ שֶׁל הַתַּלְמִיד שֶׁיִּהְיֶה כְּלִי לְקַבָּלָה,

וַהֲגַם דְּזֶהוּ עִנְיָן חִיצוֹנִי הִנֵּה חִיצוֹנִיּוּת זוֹ זֶהוּ הַקְּדָמָה אֶל הַפְּנִימִיּוּת, דְּעַל יְדֵי קֵירוּב זֶה שֶׁל הָרַב לוֹמַר לָהֶם מִלְתָא דִּבְדִיחוּתָא דְּעַל יְדֵי זֶה דַּוְקָא יוּכְלוּ לְקַבֵּל הַהַשְׁפָּעָה פְּנִימִית דְּפָתַח בִּשְׁמַעְתָּא.

וְעַל דֶּרֶךְ מָשָׁל[55] בֶּן יָנִיק וְקָטָן כְּשֶׁאָבִיו רוֹצֶה לְהִשְׁתַּעֲשֵׁעַ עִמּוֹ פָּנִים אֶל פָּנִים, וַהֲרֵי הַתִּינוֹק הוּא קָטָן, צָרִיךְ הָאָב לְהַשְׁפִּיל אֶת יָדָיו שֶׁהֵם גְּבוֹהִים וְנַעֲלִים מֵרֹאשׁ הַתִּינוֹק עַד לְמַטָּה מִתַּחַת הַתִּינוֹק וּלְהַגְבִּיהוֹ עַד רֹאשׁוֹ שֶׁל אָב וְאָז יְדַבֵּר וְיִשְׁתַּעֲשֵׁעַ עִמּוֹ פָּנִים בְּפָנִים,

---

engage the student in a particularly deep or meaningful way, but rather touches a completely external dimension of the student. Therefore, the connection that is forged between teacher and student by the teachers' humorous remark is merely an "external" one. It is, as the discourse said earlier (end of Ch. 1), the giver "giving something of his external faculties that will touch the external faculties of the receiver."

54. All of this demonstrates that before there can be any deep, internal transmission from giver to receiver there must first be an external transmission that establishes a preliminary, basic connection between them.

The discourse now cites a second example that illustrates this concept.

55. This analogy originates from Rabbi DovBer, the Maggid of Mezeritch, in *Or Torah*, #305, and is cited on the verse (quoted at the beginning of the following chapter), *I sent to Efraim and took them upon My arms* (Hosea 11:3). See also *Likkutei Torah*, *Pinchas*, cited below, footnote 58.

(But as with the analogy above, it is not cited there in relation to the concept of *Lecha Dodi*. The discourses of *Lecha Dodi* in *Maamarei Admur Hazaken Al Maamarei Razal*, p. 455, and *Semuchim La'ad, 5680*, however, do cite this analogy in relation to *Lecha Dodi*.)

In this example, the father's act of kindness in lowering his hands is a completely external expression of the father's connection with his son; he does this just to pick up the child.

The child also does not receive anything from the actual act of his father lifting him, as there is no "giving" [on the father's part] yet. The father only "gives" to his child later, *after* he has lifted the child and actually begins playing with him.[56]

Simply, it is impossible for there to be the close, deep interaction between father and child without the child first being "raised." This is the external connection that precedes and enables the deeper, internal connection.

Summary

The discourse explains that "Before Rabbah would open [begin teaching] his students"—in order to make them into fitting "vessels" to receive his Torah teachings—"he would make a humorous remark," to raise the recipients so that they would be able to receive his teachings; "attending to a Torah scholar is greater than studying under him"; although this [humorous remark] is only an external [expression of the sage] in contrast to the deep internal transmission [of his teachings], nonetheless, it is this—specifically—that serves as a harbinger to the internal transmission, much like the father who lifts his young son so that he can play with him closely, face-to-face.

---

56. In this example, the "internal transmission" is the father's playing with his son, as this is what makes the child happy. Picking up the child is (relative to their playing) merely an "external" act for both father and child. For the father: picking up his son is a very limited interaction, one that does not *openly* express his love for his child (as playing does). For the

וַהֲרֵי הַהַמְשָׁכָה שֶׁל חֶסֶד הָאָב בְּהַשְׁפָּלַת יָדָיו הוּא חִיצוֹנִיּוּת שֶׁהוּא רַק לְהַגְבִּיהַ אֶת הַתִּינוֹק,

וְכֵן הַתִּינוֹק אֵינוֹ מְקַבֵּל שׁוּם דָּבָר בְּהַגְבָּהָה זוֹ, כִּי הֲלֹא לֹא יֵשׁ בָּזֶה שׁוּם הַשְׁפָּעָה, דְּהַשְׁפָּעָה וְהַשַּׁעֲשׁוּעִים עִם בְּנוֹ הוּא רַק אַחַר כַּךְ כַּאֲשֶׁר כְּבָר הִגְבִּיהוּ,

וְרַק שֶׁאִי אֶפְשָׁר לִהְיוֹת הַהַשְׁפָּעָה בְּקֵירוּב וּבִפְנִימִיּוּת שֶׁלֹּא יִהְיֶה תְּחִלָּה קֵירוּב וַעֲלִיַּת הַמְקַבֵּל, שֶׁהוּא הַקֵּירוּב הַחִיצוֹנִי שֶׁהוּא בִּשְׁבִיל הַהַשְׁפָּעָה פְּנִימִית.

קִיצוּר.

יְבָאֵר הָא דְּרַבָּה מִקַּמֵּי דְּפָתַח לְהוּ לְרַבָּנָן לַעֲשׂוֹתָם כֵּלִים רְאוּיִם לְקַבֵּל אֶת דְּבַר הַהַשְׁפָּעָה בַּתּוֹרָה אָמַר לָהֶם מִילְתָא דִּבְדִיחוּתָא לְהַעֲלוֹת אֶת הַמְקַבְּלִים שֶׁיּוּכְלוּ לְקַבֵּל אֶת דְּבַר הַהַשְׁפָּעָה, וּגְדוֹלָה שְׁמוּשָׁהּ יוֹתֵר מִלִּימוּדָהּ, וַהֲגַם שֶׁהוּא עִנְיָן חִיצוֹנִי לְגַבֵּי פְּנִימִיּוּת הַהַשְׁפָּעָה, אֲבָל מִכָּל מָקוֹם הִנֵּה זֶהוּ דַּוְקָא הַקְדָּמָה אֶל הַפְּנִימִיּוּת, כְּדוּגְמַת הָאָב הַמֵּרִים אֶת בְּנוֹ הַקָּטָן לְהִשְׁתַּעֲשֵׁעַ עִמּוֹ בְּקֵירוּב פָּנִים בְּפָנִים.

---

child: the child does not (necessarily) sense his father's love in the act of picking up; the child merely sees that he or she is being brought closer to the father (and may not even realize that it is the father that is picking him or her up). Only later, when they actually play together, does the child feel the father's love.

3.

This is the meaning of the verse, *I sent to Efraim*[57] *and took them upon My arms* (Hosea 11[:3])[58]:

The One who is called "I am who I am"[59]—i.e., G-d Himself[60]—lowered his innermost will[61] specifically into physical *mitzvot*. And he did this in order to raise the souls of the Jewish people.[62]

DAY AND NIGHT

Man is a microcosm.[63] Just as within the larger world there is day and night—the difference between them being that during the day the light shines, as it is written, *G-d called to the light: "Day,"*[64] while during the night there is an absence of light, as it is written, *And to the darkness He called: "Night"*[63]—the same is true within a person, in a spiritual sense: there is "day" and there is "night."[65] As it is written, *Though I sit in darkness, G-d is a light unto me.*[66]

This physical world is called "darkness," since it is a world

---

57. I.e., the Children of Israel.

58. The example cited at the end of the previous chapter (of the father who lowers his hands to pick up his child so that they can play together) exists also in the relationship between G-d and the souls of the Jewish people (who are G-d's "children")—as demonstrated in this verse, where the prophet Hosea speaks of G-d drawing the Jewish people close to Him in terms of a father picking up his child in his arms. See *Likkutei Torah, Pinchas* 80b.

59. See *Ibn Ezra* to Genesis 27:19.

60. See below, note 72, that the various divine names mentioned in Scripture each express a different aspect or attribute of the Divinity. G-d Himself, however, is completely beyond

any attributes, and cannot be defined in (and limited by) those terms. G-d Himself therefore has no "name," and is instead referred to in Scripture in the first person "I"—"I am who I am," beyond any descriptions (and limitations). See *Zohar* III:11a and 257b; *Likkutei Torah*, ibid.

61. *Penimiyut haratzon*, in the Hebrew. There are two types of will: *penimiyut haratzon* (innermost will), and *chitzoniyut haratzon* (outer, or external, will). The former refers to that which one *really* desires, whereas the latter refers to that which one desires for an incidental reason.

A deeper distinction between the two: one's very *essence* is invested in seeing one's innermost will being fulfilled; for one's external will, however, while one will take the necessary steps to ensure that his desire is procured,

ג.

וְזֶהוּ[סג] דִּכְתִיב וְאָנֹכִי תִרְגַּלְתִּי לְאֶפְרַיִם קָחָם עַל זְרוֹעוֹתָיו
(הוֹשֵׁעַ י"א[סד])

דְּאָנֹכִי מִי שֶׁאָנֹכִי בָּרוּךְ הוּא הִשְׁפִּיל פְּנִימִיּוּת רְצוֹנוֹ
יִתְבָּרֵךְ בְּמִצְוֹת גַּשְׁמִיּוֹת דַּוְקָא בִּכְדֵי לְהַגְבִּיהַּ נִשְׁמוֹת יִשְׂרָאֵל,

דְּהִנֵּה[סה] הָאָדָם הוּא עוֹלָם קָטָן[כה], וּכְמוֹ שֶׁבָּעוֹלָם הֲרֵי
יֵשׁ יוֹם וָלַיְלָה דְּבַיּוֹם מֵאִיר הָאוֹר כְּמוֹ שֶׁכָּתוּב[סט] וַיִּקְרָא
אֱלֹקִים לָאוֹר יוֹם, וּבְהֶעְדֵּר הָאוֹר הוּא לַיְלָה[ל] כְּמוֹ
שֶׁכָּתוּב[סט] וְלַחֹשֶׁךְ קָרָא לָיְלָה, כֵּן הוּא בָּאָדָם גַּם כֵּן בְּרוּחָנִיּוּת
דְּיֵשׁ בּוֹ יוֹמָם וָלַיְלָה וּכְמוֹ שֶׁכָּתוּב[לא] גַּם כִּי אֵשֵׁב בַּחֹשֶׁךְ הוי'
אוֹר לִי,

חֹשֶׁךְ הוּא הָעוֹלָם הַזֶּה, דְּהָעוֹלָם הַזֶּה נִקְרָא חֹשֶׁךְ לְפִי

---

he will nonetheless not be mean-ingfully invested in seeing it through.

62. In the aforementioned example of father and child, in order for the father to play face to face with the child he must first lower his hands to pick up the child. The same is true in the relationship between G-d and the souls of the Jewish people: G-d "lowers" Himself, so to speak, to lift up the souls of the Jewish people and draw them close to Him, so that they may be "face to face" with Him.

What does G-d do to "lower" Himself? He invests His deepest, in-nermost will—a will that stems from His pure Essence—in physical mitz-vot that involve worldly matters. And He does this for only one purpose: so that the souls of the Jewish people, who have descended into this physical world and exist within a coarse body,

in a place that is far from spirituality and G-dliness, can connect with their Creator by studying Torah and ful-filling physical mitzvot.

63. *Avot d'Rabbi Nattan* 31:3; *Tan-chuma, Pekudei* 3; *Tikkunei Zohar*, 69 (100b; 101a). Every single person is a microcosm, a "small world." This means that elements and phenomena that we perceive in the world at large also exist within us, albeit on a small-er, more personal scale.

64. Genesis 1:5.

65. This topic is discussed at length in *Likkutei Torah*, ibid., 79d.

66. Micah 7:8. I.e., even in this phys-ical world, which is spiritually "dark," G-d is a "light" unto the Jewish peo-ple (*Likkutei Torah*, ibid.).

filled with falsehood and deception. When it is physically dark, one cannot see anything at all; one may even be oblivious to the fact that he is standing at the edge of a deep pit or near some other dangerous thing. The same is true of this physical world: one cannot be sure of what another person's feelings are toward him.[67] The person may express one type of sentiment with his mouth, yet feel completely different in his heart.[68] The person may honor him with his mouth, speaking to him with words of affection, and yet hate him in his heart.

Thus, this physical world is called "darkness," since it is a world filled with falsehood and deception. And whereas the World to Come is called the "world of truth," this world is called the "world of falsehood."[69]

This is the meaning of the verse, *Though I sit in darkness, G-d is a light unto me*: Even in this [dark] physical world, G-d is a light unto the Jewish people, as it is written, *For, behold, darkness may cover the earth and a thick cloud [may cover] the kingdoms, but upon you G-d* (Havaya[70]) *will shine.*[71]

Now, it is well known that the divine name *Elokim*[72] is numerically equivalent to the word *hateva* (nature),[73] while

---

67. See *Pesachim* 54b: "Seven things are hidden from mankind: The day of one's death; the day of one's comfort (when he will find relief from his hardships—*Rashi*); the true repercussions of one's deeds (or the extent of G-d's judgment in the Future—*Rashi*); one does not know what lies in another's heart; one does not know how he will earn his livelihood; when the royal House of David will return [to glory]; and when the evil [Roman] Empire will fall."

68. See ibid. 113b: "There are three types of behavior G-d despises: One who expresses one type of sentiment with his mouth, yet feels completely different in his heart...."

69. The reason why this world is a "world of falsehood," where people can deceive each other and can speak one way while feeling completely different, is because the coarse physicality of this world obscures G-dliness. Indeed, in a place where G-dliness is manifest, there is no possibility of falsehood. Hence, the World to Come—a place where the divine presence radiates—is a "world of truth."

70. See below, note 72.

71. Isaiah 60:2. This is the idea of G-d "raising" the souls of the Jewish people (mentioned above): even while they are in this physical world—a world of darkness and deception—the divine name *Havaya* shines upon

שֶׁהוּא עוֹלָם הַשֶּׁקֶר וּכְמוֹ בַּחֹשֶׁךְ הֲרֵי אֵין הָאָדָם רוֹאֶה
מְאוּמָה וְיָכוֹל לִהְיוֹת שֶׁהוּא עוֹמֵד בְּסָמוּךְ לְבוֹר אוֹ לִשְׁאָר
דָּבָר הַמַּזִּיק, הִנֵּה כְּמוֹ כֵן בָּעוֹלָם הַזֶּה אֵין אָדָם יוֹדֵעַ מַה
שֶּׁבְּלִבּוֹ שֶׁל חֲבֵירוֹ עָלָיו⁷², וְאֶפְשָׁר לִהְיוֹת אֶחָד בַּפֶּה וְאֶחָד
בַּלֵּב⁷³ דִּבְפִיו יְכַבֵּד אוֹתוֹ וּמְדַבֵּר עִמּוֹ דִּבְרֵי אַהֲבָה וּבְלִבּוֹ
הוּא שׂוֹנֵא לוֹ,

וְזֶהוּ מַה שֶּׁהָעוֹלָם הַזֶּה נִקְרָא חֹשֶׁךְ לְפִי שֶׁהוּא עוֹלָם
הַשֶּׁקֶר, דְּעוֹלָם הַבָּא נִקְרָא עוֹלָם הָאֱמֶת וְעוֹלָם הַזֶּה נִקְרָא
עָלְמָא דְשִׁיקְרָא,

וְזֶהוּ גַּם כִּי אֵשֵׁב בַּחֹשֶׁךְ הוי' אוֹר לִי דַּאֲפִילוּ בָּעוֹלָם
הַזֶּה הַגַּשְׁמִי הוי' מֵאִיר בְּיִשְׂרָאֵל כְּמוֹ שֶׁכָּתוּב⁷⁴ כִּי הִנֵּה
הַחֹשֶׁךְ יְכַסֶּה אֶרֶץ וַעֲרָפֶל לְאוּמִים וְעָלַיִךְ יִזְרַח הוי',

וְיָדוּעַ דֶאלקים בְּגִימַטְרִיָּא הַטֶּבַע⁷⁵, וַהוי' הוּא הָיָה הֹוֶה

---

them. See following footnote.

72. HAVAYA/ELOKIM. *Havaya* and *El-okim* are two of the seven primary divine names mentioned in Scripture. (*Havaya* is the colloquial form—in Kabbalah and *Chakirah* (Torah philosophy)—of the Ineffable Divine Name, or Tetragrammaton, Y-H-V-H. The letters are rearranged so as not to pronounce the sacred Name.)

Each divine name expresses a different aspect or attribute of the Divinity (see *Shemot Rabbah* 3:6).

The name of *Keil*, for example, refers to G-d in His attribute of kindness, *Elokim* refers to G-d in His attribute of justice, while *Havaya* refers to G-d in His attribute of mercy (see *Rashi* to Genesis 1:1).

Chasidus explains the difference between *Havaya* and *Elokim* thus:

Havaya refers to G-d the Infinite, transcending creation and nature, time and space completely—the level of Divinity that brings everything into existence *ex nihilo*. The name *El-okim* represents the level of G-dliness which conceals the infinite light and life-force, as this infinite force is too intense for finite creatures to endure. *Elokim* is the power of G-d that makes the world appear as though it exists naturally and independently by itself. *Elokim* therefore has the same numerical value as the Hebrew word for "nature"—*hateva*.

73. *Pardes, Shaar* 12 (*Shaar Ha-netivot*), Ch. 2; *Reishit Chochmah, Shaar Hateshuvah,* Ch. 6 (121b); *Shaloh* 89a, 189a, 308b; *She'elot u'Teshuvot Chacham Tzvi* 18; *Shaar Hayichud Veha'emunah,* Ch. 6, beg.

the divine name *Havaya*[72] connotes the fact that G-d contains past, present and future simultaneously[74]—i.e., the dimension of G-dliness that transcends nature.[75] Hence, *darkness may cover the earth*, as the nations can only perceive nature; *but upon you G-d* (Havaya) *will shine*, the dimension of G-dliness that transcends nature.[76]

SPIRITUAL LIGHT AND DARKNESS

In terms of a person's spiritual service: When one's soul[77] permeates his being and its force shines within him it is called "day"; but when his soul does not shine within him it is then called "night."

Therefore, at night, when the soul departs from the body, a person is in a state of complete sleep. In the morning, G-d returns his soul, as it is written, *They are new every morning; great is Your faithfulness!*[78]

But since the body's life force is exceedingly coarse, a person can only embrace a very minute amount of the soul's radiance.[79]

This is the meaning of the phrase, "*who has the soul in his*

---

74. See *Zohar* I:257b; *Pardes, Shaar* 1 (*Shaar Eser V'lo Tesha*), Ch. 9; *Shaar Hayichud Veha'emunah*, Ch. 4 and 7.

75. See *Sefer Hamaamarim 5679*, p. 360; *Sefer Hamaamarim Kuntresim*, vol. 1, p. 97a ff.; *Sefer Hamaamarim 5697*, p. 149.

76. Our physical world appears to be dictated not by a supernatural G-dly force, but rather by the very predictable laws of "nature." Indeed, Divinity is not readily evident in nature. This is because the world is created with the divine name *Elokim*, whose function is to *conceal* the supernatural G-dly force (*Havaya*). (As Scripture states (Genesis 1:1), *Bereishit bara Elokim—In the beginning, Elokim creat-*

ed....) In the words of Rabbi Schneur Zalman of Liadi (*Shaar Hayichud Veha'emunah*, Ch. 6, beg.): "*Elokim*... conceals the Supernal Light that brings the world into existence and gives it life; and it appears as though the world exists and conducts itself in a natural way." This world is thus called a world of "darkness" (*darkness may cover the earth*), since the supernatural G-dly light is hidden and concealed.

It is only upon the Children of Israel, who are not subject to the concealment of *Elokim*, that the supernatural dimension of G-dliness —*Havaya*—"shines."

The discourse has thus explained the spiritual meaning of "day" and "night" in the context of the world at

וְיִהְיֶה כְּאֶחָד[ל] שֶׁהוּא לְמַעֲלָה מִן הַטֶּבַע, וְזֶהוּ כִּי הַחֹשֶׁךְ יְכַסֶּה
אֶרֶץ שֶׁהֵם יוֹדְעִים רַק עִנְיְנֵי הַטִּבְעִי[ל], אֲבָל עָלַיִךְ יִזְרַח הוי'
שֶׁהוּא לְמַעֲלָה מִן הַטֶּבַע.

וּבַעֲבוֹדָה הוּא דְּכַאֲשֶׁר נִשְׁמַת הָאָדָם מִתְפַּשֶּׁטֶת בּוֹ וְאוֹר
כֹּחַ נִשְׁמָתוֹ מְאִירָה לוֹ אֲזַי נִקְרָא יוֹם, וְכַאֲשֶׁר אוֹר
נִשְׁמָתוֹ בִּלְתִּי מְאִירָה לוֹ חַס וְשָׁלוֹם אָז הוּא נִקְרָא לַיְלָה,

לָכֵן בַּלַּיְלָה הוּא בִּבְחִינַת שֵׁינָה לְגַמְרֵי מֵחֲמַת הִסְתַּלְקוּת
אוֹר נַפְשׁוֹ וּבַבֹּקֶר הַקָּדוֹשׁ בָּרוּךְ הוּא מַחֲזִיר לְהָאָדָם
נִשְׁמָתוֹ וּכְמוֹ שֶׁכָּתוּב[לח] חֲדָשִׁים לַבְּקָרִים רַבָּה אֱמוּנָתֶךָ,

אַךְ מֵחֲמַת שֶׁנִּתְגַּשֵּׁם חַיּוּת הַגּוּף מְאֹד אֵינוּ יָכוֹל לְקַבֵּל
הֶאָרַת נִשְׁמָתוֹ בְּקִרְבּוֹ כִּי אִם מְעַט מִזְעֵיר,

וְזֶהוּ אֲשֶׁר נִשְׁמָה בְּאַפּוֹ[לט], דְּהַיְינוּ שֶׁהַנְּשָׁמָה הָאֱלֹקִית אֵין

---

large ("day" referring to when the dimension of G-dliness that transcends nature is manifest, "night" referring to when this force is concealed and hidden). The discourse now turns its attention to the "small world," explaining the concepts of "day" and "night" as they relate to a person's divine service.

77. I.e., one's G-dly soul, which is "literally a part of G-d above" (*Tanya*, Ch. 2, beg.). The terms "day" and "night" thus refer to the distinction between when one's G-dly soul is manifest and active and when it is subdued and inactive.

78. Lamentations 3:23. See *Yalkut Shimoni, Tehillim, Remez* 702; *Shul-*

chan Aruch Harav, Orach Chaim (Mahadura Kama) 4:1.

The spiritual concepts of "day" and "night" are connected with the *physical* times of day and night. At night, when a person sleeps, his soul *departs* from the body—the very idea of spiritual "night." And in the morning (day) G-d returns the soul to the person—the idea of spiritual "day" (manifestation of the soul).

79. The severe coarseness of the body naturally obscures the soul's radiance. Therefore, when a person wakes up in the morning and his body is at its full strength, it is impossible for the soul to fully express itself within the body. Rather, only a small "glimmer" of the soul's radiance can be manifest.

nostrils"[80]: in the morning, before a person prays, the G-dly soul cannot radiate within his heart and body, since the body is so coarse.[81]

Prayer is connection[82]—through prayer one connects with G-d. Regarding one's status before prayer, i.e., before one connects with G-d through his divine service, it is written, *Withdraw from man who has the soul in his nostrils, for with what* (bameh) *is he deemed [worthy]?*[83] Our Sages commented on this verse, "Do not read the word as *bameh* ('with what'), but rather as *bamah* ('a platform')."[84]

The verse is thus interpreted as follows:[85] *Withdraw from [man]*—separate yourself from a person whose soul lies only in his nostrils, one whose soul has yet to permeate his entire body, for he is deemed a *bamah*, a platform.

A platform is something that is physically high, something that appears as a separate entity. Similarly, one who has not yet prayed is a being that is independent and separate [from G-d][86]—until he prays, which is the idea of "connection," when he connects with G-dliness. And through prayer one transforms physical objects into conduits for G-dliness.[87]

Now, in order for there to be this deep, internal connection [between G-d and man], to the extent that one even elic-

---

80. This phrase comes from the verse (in Isaiah) cited below. See *Ramaz* on *Zohar* II:182a (cited in *Likkutei Torah*, ibid.); *Zohar Chadash, Rut*, 90d. See also the sources cited below, note 85.

81. So long as one has yet to recite the morning prayers, the soul is "in his *nostrils*": a person may acknowledge G-d in the mind and intellect, but the heart remains devoid of G-dliness (*Likkutei Torah*, ibid.).

82. The Hebrew word for prayer is *tefillah*. The etymological root of *tefillah* (תפילה) is *tafal* (תפל), which

means to "paste" or "bind." (See *Torah Or, Terumah* 79d, et al. See also *Torat Menachem—Hitvaaduyot 5712*, vol. 7, p. 17, fn. 8.) In a deeper sense, then, the "service of prayer" (*tefillah*) entails toiling (during prayer) to *bind* and *connect* oneself with G-d.

83. Isaiah 2:22.

84. *Berachot* 14a.

85. *Likkutei Torah*, ibid.; *Maamarei Admur Hazaken Al Parshiyot Hatorah*, p. 747; *Maamarei Admur Hazaken Al Maamarei Razal*, p. 17; *Derech Chaim, Shaar Hatefillah*, Ch. 83; *Or*

לָהּ גִּילוּי בְּלִבּוֹ וְגוּפוֹ מֵחֲמַת חוֹמֶר יֵשׁוּת הַגּוּף כֵּיוָן
שֶׁעֲדַיִין לֹא הִתְפַּלֵּל,

דִּתְפִלָּה הוּא עִנְיַן הַתְקַשְּׁרוּתוּ, וְקוֹדֶם הַתְּפִלָּה הַיְינוּ
קוֹדֶם שֶׁהָאָדָם מִתְקַשֵּׁר לֵאלֹקוּת עַל יְדֵי עֲבוֹדָה כְּתִיב בּוּמא
חִדְלוּ לָכֶם מִן הָאָדָם אֲשֶׁר נְשָׁמָה בְּאַפּוֹ כִּי בַּמֶּה נֶחְשָׁב הוּא,
אַל תִּקְרֵי בַּמֶּה אֶלָּא בָּמָה,

פֵּירוּשׁמג חִדְלוּ לָכֶם, הִבָּדְלוּ עַצְמְכֶם מִן בְּחִינַת אָדָם כָּזֶה
שֶׁנִּשְׁמָתוֹ רַק בְּאַפִּיוּמג, שֶׁלֹּא נִתְפַּשְּׁטָה עוֹד נִשְׁמָתוֹ בְּכָל
גּוּפוֹ, כִּי בַּמֶּה נֶחְשָׁב, שֶׁהוּא נֶחְשָׁב כְּמוֹ בָּמָה,

וּכְשֵׁם שֶׁהַבָּמָה הוּא דָּבָר גָּבוֹהַּ וְנִרְאָה הַיֵּשׁוּת שֶׁלּוֹ לְדָבָר
בִּפְנֵי עַצְמוֹ כֵּן הָאָדָם הַזֶּה הוּא עוֹד יֵשׁ וּמְצִיאוּת עַד אֲשֶׁר
מִתְפַּלֵּל שֶׁהוּא עִנְיַן הַהִתְקַשְּׁרוּת שֶׁמִּתְקַשֵּׁר בֵּאלֹקוּת וְעַל יְדֵי
הַתְּפִלָּה עוֹשֶׂה כָּל הַדְּבָרִים הַגַּשְׁמִים כֵּלִים לֵאלֹקוּת,

וּבִכְדֵי שֶׁיִּהְיֶה הַקֵּירוּב פְּנִימִי לְהַמְשִׁיךְ הָאוֹר הָאֱלֹקִי
בְּכָל הָעִנְיָנִים הַגַּשְׁמִים צָרִיךְ לִהְיוֹת תְּחִלָּה הַקֵּירוּב כְּלָלִי,

---

Hatorah, Bereshit, vol. 6, p. 1020a.

86. Before one connects with G-dliness (through prayer), he senses only his own being and existence, thus perceiving himself to be an independent entity from G-d.

87. The purpose of the service of prayer, as explained above, is to connect oneself with G-dliness to the point that the radiance of one's soul permeates his entire being. When this happens, when the holiness of the soul is felt within even the coarse physical body, then all of one's mundane *actions* will similarly be permeated with a holy purpose. One will

eat and drink not to satisfy his base cravings, but rather to energize himself so that he may study more Torah and fulfill *mitzvot*; one will involve himself in business matters not for greedy purposes, but rather so that he will be able to assist those who are less fortunate than him.

And all of this represents the Jewish people's "internal connection" with G-dliness (mentioned above): the radiance of one's G-dly soul permeates one's entire body, so that the body is filled with the soul's holiness, and all of one's mundane actions are directed toward the service of G-d, filling them with a G-dly purpose and meaning.

its G-dliness within all of his physical matters, there must first be a more general [external] connection. This is why our Sages say that "only with a sense of earnestness may one begin to pray"[88]—which *Rashi* explains as referring to the quality of surrender and humility[89]—for this establishes the initial, general connection [between man and G-d].

A WOMAN'S BLESSING

This, then, is the meaning of *Come, my Beloved, to meet the bride*[90]—it is the giver drawing close to the receiver [to create an external connection, so that ultimately the receiver will be ready for the deeper, internal connection]. But through this [internal connection the giver actually *gains* from the receiver, as it says] *let us **welcome** the Shabbat* [i.e., *receive* from Shabbat], as "all the days [of the subsequent week] are blessed from Shabbat."[91] This is much like the relationship between teacher and student, where "I have learned much from my teachers... but from my students I learned more than from all the others."[92] Similarly, it is written, *An accomplished woman is the crown of her husband.*[93] It is also written, *One who has found a wife has found goodness, and has brought forth favor from G-d*[94] Who is good—with [a blessing for] offspring that are upright and blessed, children and grandchildren who are occupied with Torah and *mitzvot*.

Summary

The discourse explains that this is the idea of G-d lowering His innermost will into physical *mitzvot*; man is a microcosm; this [physical] world is called "darkness," as it is a "world of falsehood"; when one's soul shines within him through his

---

88. *Berachot* 5:1.

89. See *Rashi* to *Berachot* 30b, s.v. *koved rosh*. I.e., before a person begins praying to G-d he must surrender his ego and be humbled before Whom he stands.

90. The discourse now returns to the discussion begun in Chapter 1, and describes how the concepts of "internal" and "external" connections relate to a groom and bride, and to the welcoming of Shabbat.

וְלָכֵן אֵין עוֹמְדִין לְהִתְפַּלֵּל אֶלָּא מִתּוֹךְ כּוֹבֶד רֹאשׁ[מד] וּפֵרֵשׁ
רַשׁ״י הַכְנָעָה וְשִׁפְלוּת[מה] שֶׁהוּא עִנְיַן הַקֵּירוּב הַכְּלָלִי.

וְזֶהוּ לְכָה דוֹדִי לִקְרַאת כַּלָּה[מו] קֵירוּב הַמַּשְׁפִּיעַ אֶל
הַמְקַבֵּל, הִנֵּה עַל יְדֵי זֶה פְּנֵי שַׁבָּת נְקַבְּלָה דְּכָל הַיָּמִים
מִתְבָּרְכִין מֵהַשַּׁבָּת, וְעַל דֶּרֶךְ בְּהַשְׁפָּעַת הָרַב וְתַלְמִיד דְּהַרְבֵּה
קִבַּלְתִּי מֵרַבּוֹתַי כו׳ וּמִתַּלְמִידַי יוֹתֵר מִכּוּלָּם[מז], וְכֵן כְּתִיב[מח]
אֵשֶׁת חַיִל עֲטֶרֶת בַּעְלָהּ, וּכְתִיב[מט] מָצָא אִשָּׁה מָצָא טוֹב וְיָפִיקוּ
רָצוֹן מֵה׳ הַטּוֹב בְּדוֹר יְשָׁרִים יְבוֹרָךְ בְּבָנִים וּבְנֵי בָנִים
עוֹסְקִים בַּתּוֹרָה וּמִצְוֹת.

קִיצוּר.

יְבָאֵר כִּי זֶהוּ עִנְיַן מַה שֶׁהוּא יִתְבָּרֵךְ הִשְׁפִּיל פְּנִימִיּוּת
רְצוֹנוֹ יִתְבָּרֵךְ בְּמִצְוֹת מַעֲשִׂיּוֹת, כִּי הָאָדָם עוֹלָם קָטָן
וְהָעוֹלָם הַזֶּה נִקְרָא חֹשֶׁךְ כִּי הוּא עָלְמָא דְשִׁיקְרָא, וְכַאֲשֶׁר

---

91. As explained above (Ch. 1), Shabbat is likened to a queen, which alludes to the fact that although it appears to be the "receiver" (in its relationship with the "giver"—"my Beloved"), it actually fulfills the giver through their union, and ultimately is the source of supernal blessings, *giving* blessings to the "giver."

92. *Taanit* 7a. Although within the teacher/student relationship it appears as though the teacher is the only "giver," giving of his wisdom to his students, they in fact give to him, as the teacher gains the deepest wisdom

through teaching his students.

93. Proverbs 12:4. This same concept applies to every groom and bride: The groom *receives* from the bride, as she is called *the crown of her husband*.

94. Ibid. 18:22. I.e., although the wife (bride) is the "receiver," she is ultimately the true source of all the blessings, as mentioned above (Ch. 1). See also *Or Hatorah, Nach*, vol. 1, p. 615 ff., where it is explained that *One who has found a wife has found goodness* specifically because of the superiority of the "receiver."

spiritual service it is called "day"; when one has not performed his spiritual service it is called "night," and he is referred to as one whose *soul is in his nostrils*—of whom the
verse warns *Withdraw from* [a] *man* such as this who is like a
bamah (platform), i.e., a separate, independent being; one is
drawn close to G-dliness through prayer, which is "connection"; [through prayer] one is then able to connect all of his
physical matters with G-dliness, in complete unity.

אוֹר נִשְׁמַת הָאָדָם מְאִירָה בּוֹ בַּעֲבוֹדָה נִקְרָא יוֹם, וּבְהֶעָדֵר
הָעֲבוֹדָה נִקְרָא לַיְלָה וְנִקְרָא נְשָׁמָה בְּאַפּוֹ שֶׁעָלָיו נֶאֱמַר
חִדְלוּ לָכֶם מִן הָאָדָם זֶה שֶׁהוּא כְּמוֹ בָּמָה שֶׁהוּא יֵשׁ, וְהַקֵּירוּב
לֵאלֹקוּת הוּא עַל יְדֵי תְפִלָּה שֶׁהוּא עִנְיַן הַהִתְקַשְּׁרוּת דְּאָז
בִּיכוֹלְתּוֹ לְקַשֵּׁר כָּל הָעִנְיָנִים הַגַּשְׁמִים בֵּאלֹקוּת בְּיִחוּד
גָּמוּר.

With the Help of Heaven
Shabbat Parshat Teitzei, 13 Elul, 5714

Come, my Beloved, to meet the bride; let us welcome the Shabbat.[1]

SPIRITUAL GROOM AND BRIDE

In his discourse of *Lecha Dodi* (from the wedding discourses[2]), my father-in-law, the Rebbe, cites the idea (from *Pirkei d'Rabbi Eliezer*[3]) that "a groom is likened to a king," and a bride to a queen.[4] [In a spiritual sense,] "groom" refers to G-d, and "bride" refers to the Jewish people.[5] Within the *sefirot* they refer to *z'eyr anpin*[6] and *malchut*[7]—"groom" is *z'eyr anpin*, and "bride" is *malchut*.[8]

---

1. This is the opening line of the *Lecha Dodi* hymn, composed by Rabbi Shlomo HaLevi Alkabetz, 16th-century Kabbalist, and sung every Friday night in the *Kabbalat Shabbat* service.

The commentaries explain that this passage is the Jewish people's invitation to G-d (*my Beloved*) to join in ushering in the Shabbat (*bride*).

2. In 5689 (1928), at the wedding of Rabbi Menachem M. Schneerson and Rebbetzin Chaya Mushka, of blessed memory, the bride's father, Rabbi Yosef Yitzchak Schneersohn, then Lubavitcher Rebbe, delivered a Chasidic discourse on the opening line of *Lecha Dodi*. In 5714 (1954), Rabbi Menachem M. Schneerson, who succeeded his father-in-law as Rebbe in 5710 (1950), delivered the present discourse as an exposition of that discourse. Rabbi Yosef Yitzchak's discourse was printed in *Sefer Hamaamarim Kuntresim*, vol. 1, p. 20a ff. In the year 5739 (1979), it was re-

printed in booklet form, commemorating the fiftieth anniversary of the wedding. Additionally, it appears in *Sefer Hamaamarim 5689*, p. 81 ff.

3. Chapter 16.

4. Both Shabbat and a bride are referred to by our Sages with the appellation "queen." This indicates that (in a deeper sense) there is a correlation between the concepts of Shabbat and a bride, as discussed at length in *Lecha Dodi, 5689*.

5. See Song of Songs 3:11, and *Taanit* 26b: *On His wedding day*—"this is the Giving of the Torah." Just as a wedding facilitates the union of a man and a woman, so did the Giving of the Torah facilitate a union between G-d and the Jewish people. Within this union, G-d is called the "groom," as He is the Giver, and the Jewish people are called the "bride," being the receiver. See below, fn. 8.

בס"ד. ש"פ תצא, י"ג אלול, ה'תשי"ד.

לְכָה דוֹדִי לִקְרַאת כַּלָּה פְּנֵי שַׁבָּת נְקַבְּלָה,

וּמֵבִיא כְּבוֹד קְדֻשַּׁת מוֹרִי וְחָמִי אַדְמוּ"ר בְּמַאֲמָרוֹ לְכָה
דוֹדִי (מִדְּרוּשֵׁי הַחֲתוּנָה⁎) (מִפִּרְקֵי דְרַבִּי אֱלִיעֶזֶר⁎) שֶׁחָתָן
דּוֹמֶה לְמֶלֶךְ וְהַכַּלָּה לְמַלְכָּה. חָתָן זֶה הַקָּדוֹשׁ בָּרוּךְ הוּא
וְכַלָּה הִיא כְּנֶסֶת יִשְׂרָאֵל, וּבַסְּפִירוֹת הוּא עִנְיַן זָ"א וּמַלְכוּת,
דְּחָתָן הוּא בְּחִינַת זָ"א וְכַלָּה הִיא בְּחִינַת מַלְכוּת.

---

6. Z'EYR ANPIN. Literally, "small face," this is the Kabbalistic term used collectively for the six *middot* or *sefirot* of *chesed*, *gevurah*, *tiferet*, *netzach*, *hod*, and *yesod*. It is often abbreviated as *z'a*.

7. MALCHUT. Literally, royalty or kingship; the tenth and last of the *sefirot*. *Malchut* is referred to in the *Tikkunei Zohar* (intro. 17a) as the "Mouth of G-d," the Word or Speech of G-d by which the world comes into actual being. (Both mouth and speech are used for communication with "others" outside of self.) The world and the created beings (the "others") make it possible for there to be a divine kingdom, since "there cannot be a king without a nation," i.e., G-d cannot be a ruler without the existence of the element of "other."

Eitz Chaim (6:5, 8:5, et passim) speaks of *malchut* as being "a dim speculum, because it has no (light) of its own." The *Zohar* (I:249b, 251b) therefore compares *malchut* to "the moon that has no light of its own save that which is given to it from the sun." Paradoxically, although *malchut*

is a passive *sefirah* that only contains that which the other *sefirot* pour into it, it is specifically through *malchut* that the original creative plan is actualized, as will be elaborated below in the discourse.

8. Since physical man is created in the "image" of the *sefirot*, it follows that the physical concept of king and queen has a spiritual counterpart—a concept of "king" and "queen" within the *sefirot* (*Lecha Dodi, 5689*).

To explain: Every soul consists of two parts, masculine and feminine. Born from a union between *z'a* and *malchut* of *Atzilut*, the soul's masculine part—the "active transmitter" of divine light—has its source in *z'a*, while the feminine part—the "passive recipient"—has its source in *malchut*. "Masculine" and "feminine" also refer to "root" and "revelation": the soul's root is in *z'a*, and its revelation in *malchut*. The male aspect, *z'a*, is called "king," while the female aspect, *malchut*, is called "queen" (*Yom Tov Shel Rosh Hashanah 5666*, new edition, p. 207).

The relationship between *z'a* and

This, then, is the [deeper] meaning of *Come, my Beloved, to meet the bride; let us welcome the Shabbat*: it refers to the transmission [of G-dly light] from *z'a* to *malchut*.[9]

TRANSMISSIONS

And the order of transmission is thus: First there must be an "external" transmission (from *z'a* to *malchut*), one that is considered merely "encompassing," and this is followed by the internal transmission.[10]

Indeed, such is the order of every transmission from giver to receiver. There must first be a transmission from the external faculties of the giver to the external faculties of the receiver. This enables the receiver to rise and become close to the level of the giver, and afterwards he can receive the deeper, internal transmission from the giver.

TWO EXAMPLES

To illustrate this concept, Rabbi Yosef Yitzchak cites[11] two examples [one, of a teacher who transmits knowledge to his student, and one, of a father who plays with his young son].[12]

It can be said that his intention in citing these examples is not merely to demonstrate the *order* of the transmission (namely, that the external connection paves the way for the internal connection), but rather to (also) explain the magnitude of these two transmissions:[13]

FROM EXTERNAL TO INTERNAL

The external transmission is, indeed, of extremely lofty cal-

---

malchut parallels the (physical, intimate) relationship between a human king and queen, in which the king (male) is the transmitter and the queen (female) is the recipient.

9. I.e., the "groom" coming towards the "bride."

10. For "in order for there to be any union of giver and receiver, the receiver must 'ascend,' so as to draw close to the giver. But before this can occur, the giver must first establish an external connection with the receiver, by giving something of his external faculties that will touch the external faculties of the receiver. This in turn enables the receiver to lift himself up, to rise until he becomes close to the standing of the giver, so that he may then receive from the giver the deeper, internal transmission" (*Lecha Dodi, 5689*).

וְזֶהוּ לְכָה דוֹדִי לִקְרַאת כַּלָּה פְּנֵי שַׁבָּת נְקַבְּלָה, שֶׁהוּא עִנְיָן הַמְשָׁכַת זָ״א לְמַלְכוּת,

וְסֵדֶר הַהַמְשָׁכָה הוּא, אֲשֶׁר תְּחִלָּה צְרִיכָה לִהְיוֹת הַהַמְשָׁכָה חִיצוֹנִית (מִזָ״א לְמַלְכוּת) שֶׁהִיא רַק בִּבְחִינַת מַקִּיף, וְאַחַר כַּךְ הִיא הַהַמְשָׁכָה פְּנִימִית.

דְּכֵן הוּא הַסֵּדֶר בְּכָל הַשְׁפָּעָה מִמַּשְׁפִּיעַ לַמְקַבֵּל, דְּתְחִלָּה צְרִיכָה לִהְיוֹת הַמְשָׁכַת הַמַּשְׁפִּיעַ מִבְּחִינַת חִיצוֹנִיּוּת שֶׁלּוֹ לִבְחִינַת חִיצוֹנִיּוּת הַמְקַבֵּל, שֶׁעַל יְדֵי זֶה מִתְעַלֶּה הַמְקַבֵּל לִהְיוֹת קָרוֹב לְמַדְרֵגַת הַמַּשְׁפִּיעַ, וְאַחַר כַּךְ יוּכַל לְקַבֵּל הַמְשָׁכָה הַפְּנִימִית מֵהַמַּשְׁפִּיעַ.

וּמֵבִיא עַל זֶה[11] ב׳ מְשָׁלִים [מֵהַשְׁפָּעַת רַב לְתַלְמִיד, וְאָב הַמִּשְׁתַּעֲשֵׁעַ עִם בְּנוֹ הַקָּטָן].

וְיֵשׁ לוֹמַר, שֶׁכַּוָּנָתוֹ בִּמְשָׁלִים אֵלֶּה הִיא לֹא רַק לְהָבִיא דוּגְמָאוֹת לְסֵדֶר הַהַמְשָׁכָה (שֶׁהַהַשְׁפָּעָה חִיצוֹנִית הִיא הַקְּדָמָה לְהַהַשְׁפָּעָה פְּנִימִית), אֶלָּא (גַּם) לְבָאֵר גּוֹדֶל הָעִילּוּי שֶׁבִּב׳ הַשְׁפָּעוֹת אֵלּוּ,

דְּגַם הַהַשְׁפָּעָה חִיצוֹנִית הִיא דַרְגָּא נַעֲלֵית בְּיוֹתֵר, וְעַד

In terms of a physical wedding: The *chuppah* (wedding canopy that covers the groom and bride) allows for the union of groom and bride. But before the *chuppah* can occur, there must first be the *kabbalat panim*—"the welcoming ceremony." This is where the groom (the "giver") approaches the bride (the "receiver") and covers her face with a veil, establishing a very basic, "external" connection. This raises the bride up to a higher standing, and enables the *chuppah*, when groom and bride unite in a deeper, more internal way.

11. In **Chapter 2** of his discourse.

12. These will be (cited and) analyzed below, in Chapter 3.

13. At first glance, it may seem that an external transmission is of lesser quality than an internal one, as the former serves merely to pave the way for the latter. Here, however, the discourse argues a fundamental point, that on the contrary, the *external* transmission possesses a tremendous advantage, for it originates in a far loftier source than the internal transmission.

iber, to the extent that it is of a much greater status than the internal transmission. For the external transmission, which is a *makif*,[14] transcends the recipient's capacity (in contrast to an internal transmission, which is internalized by the recipient's capacity).[15]

Nevertheless, it merely paves the way for the inner transmission, for it is specifically through the internal transmission that one can reach an extremely greater status (one that transcends the realm of *makif*).[16]

MYSTICAL CHUPPAH

This is the meaning of, *For over all the honor there will be a* chuppah (canopy).[17] [The use of the word "*all*" here indicates that] there are two kinds of "honor" [encompassed by this *chuppah*][18]: the honor of the groom, and the honor of the bride.[19]

---

14. MAKIF. Literally, "encompassing." In Chasidic terminology, this term does not connote "encompassing" in a spatial sense, i.e., that somehow this external transmission physically surrounds the person. Rather, it is used figuratively, to indicate an element extant within the person that is not yet consciously sensed or perceived.

15. The loftiness of the external transmission is not (only) due to the low rank of the recipient, but primarily due to its *own* lofty quality. Besides the recipient's capacity being incomparably lower than the giver's, causing the transmission to remain in a *makif* state—the fact that the subject of transmission *actually transcends* the acceptance capabilities of the recipient makes it impossible for the recipient to grasp it at all.

(For example, a teacher who imparts a deep thought to his students. Since it is far too profound for their academic abilities to grasp, it remains

beyond their understanding.)

This would imply that the external transmission remains as a *makif* due to its *inherent greatness*, in contrast to the internal transmission, which can enter the person *because* of its lower level.

16. Namely, that of "essence." There are three types of transmission between giver and receiver: 1) *Pnimi*, Internal; 2) *Makif*, Encompassing; 3) *Etzem*, Essence.

To explain: 1) *Pnimi*: Transmission that can be grasped by the recipient; 2) *Makif*: Transmission that transcends the recipient's capacity, as described above in fn. 14. However, the fact that this transmission "encompasses" the specific recipient in a manner that is not consciously sensed or perceived denotes that there *does* exist *some* sense of relationship between the giver and receiver of this transmission, albeit not enough to be internally grasped; 3) *Etzem*: Totally

שֶׁיֵּשׁ בָּהּ עִילּוּי לְגַבֵּי הַהַשְׁפָּעָה פְּנִימִית. כִּי הַהַשְׁפָּעָה
חִיצוֹנִית, שֶׁהִיא בְּחִינַת מַקִּיף, הִיא לְמַעְלָה מִכְּלֵי הַמְקַבֵּל (מַה
שֶּׁאֵין כֵּן הַהַשְׁפָּעָה פְּנִימִית שֶׁמִּתְקַבֶּלֶת בִּכְלֵי הַמְקַבֵּל).

וּמִכָּל מָקוֹם הִיא רַק הַקְדָּמָה לְהַהַשְׁפָּעָה פְּנִימִית, כִּי
דַוְקָא עַל יְדֵי הַשְׁפָּעָה הַפְּנִימִית מַגִּיעִים לְעִילּוּי נַעֲלֶה יוֹתֵר
(שֶׁלְּמַעְלָה מִבְּחִינַת הַמַּקִּיף).

וְזֶהוּ עַל כָּל כָּל כָּבוֹד חוּפָּה¹ שֶׁהֵם ב' בְּחִינוֹת כָּבוֹד, כְּבוֹד
חָתָן וּכְבוֹד כַּלָּה,

---

transcending any type of revelation to the recipient.

The discourse has explained above that the external transmission is of a much higher status than the internal transmission, for the latter is tailored to the recipient's capacity. It is now asserted that the external transmission is not the ultimate; in fact, it only paves the way for the internal transmission. Thus, it is specifically through the *internal* transmission that one can reach the *essence* of the giver. This will be elaborated below.

17. **This is the text of a verse—Isaiah 4:5.** This verse in Isaiah's prophecy of the Messianic era speaks of the divine protection that will be afforded to the righteous, to protect them from the destruction that will rain down upon the wicked: *When the L-rd will have washed the filth of the daughters of Zion and rinsed the blood of Jerusalem from her midst, with a spirit of judgment and a spirit of purging. G-d will create over every structure of Mount Zion and over those who assemble in it a cloud by day, and smoke and a glow of flaming fire by night, for over all the honor there will be a* chuppah (ibid., 4-5).

Chasidus explains that there is great significance in Isaiah's use of the word *chuppah* to describe G-d's protective presence over the Jewish people—"protecting the Jewish people's honor." It indicates an aspect of G-d's presence that "covers" and unites G-d and the Jewish people, much like a wedding *chuppah* that unites groom and bride (*Likkutei Torah, Shir Hashirim,* 47b ff.; *Siddur im Dach,* 28d ff.; *Maamarei Admur Ha'emtzaei, Derushei Chatunah,* p. 1 ff.; ibid., p. 7).

18. "Honor" refers to an aspect that "encompasses," as opposed to an aspect that "permeates."

To explain: Some qualities are more internal and others more external. Knowledge, for example, is an internal quality. When one is given knowledge it enters and is collected within his mind. Honor, however, is an external quality. The honor bestowed upon a person does not enter within him, but "surrounds" him and lifts him up to a higher stature.

19. The verse's inclusion of the seemingly superfluous word "*all*" alludes to the fact that this *chuppah* "covers"

On a more sublime level,[20] these [two] correspond to the honor of *abba* and the honor of *imma*.[21] And through this [honor that transcends both of these realms] the union of *abba* and *imma* can take place, as well that of *z'a* and *nukva*.[22]

Although both of these ([i.e.] honor (and *chuppah*) of *abba* and *imma*, along with the honor (and *chuppah*) of *z'a* and *nukva*) are in a state of *makif*, nevertheless, it is a known fact[23] that it is specifically through a union of *z'a* and *nukva* (which is an internal union) that the essence can be elicited.[24]

---

more than one type of "honor"—the honor of the groom and the honor of the bride.

In *Lecha Dodi, 5689*: "The 'honor of the groom' is G-d's love of the Jewish people, as it is written (Malachi 1:2), '*I have loved you,*' says G-d. The 'honor of the bride' is the Jewish people's love of G-d, as it is written (Psalms 84:2), *My soul yearns, indeed it pines [for the courtyards of the L-rd].* And the '*chuppah*' [is an even loftier level that] generally encompasses both "groom" and "bride."

In the groom/bride relationship, it is their love for one another that encompasses, surrounds, and envelops them: the bride is completely enveloped by her groom's love, and the groom is completely enveloped by his bride's love.

The same is true in the groom/bride relationship between G-d and the Jewish people: the Jewish people are enveloped by G-d's love (the "*honor* of the groom"), and G-d is enveloped by the Jewish people's love (the "*honor* of the bride").

Both groom and bride possess aspects that are "encompassing"—their love for one another. Yet, in order for there to be the *union* of groom and bride, who are two distinct (and even

opposing) entities, an even greater encompassing force—the *chuppah*—is required. The *chuppah*, which surrounds both groom and bride, represents an encompassing G-dly light so lofty that it is capable of joining these two forces together.

20. **Regarding all this, see** *Siddur [im Dach]* **and** *Likkutei Torah, Shir Hashirim,* **s.v.** *Ki al kol kavod.*

21. ABBA and IMMA. Literally, "father and mother," these refer to *chochmah* and *binah* respectively, when in a *partzuf* state, i.e., in their integrated form, where they each contain the elements of all the other *sefirot*). *Chochmah* and *binah*, wisdom and understanding, are conceived of as the father and mother that give birth to the emotions.

It is from the union of *chochmah* and *binah* that *z'a*, the *middot* (also called *toldot*, or "offspring"), are born. *Tanya*, Chapter 3, explains this in anthropomorphic terms: "The intellect of the rational soul, which is the faculty that conceives any thing, is given the appellation *chochmah*. When one brings forth this power from the potential into the actual, that is, when a person cogitates with his intellect in

וּלְמַעְלָה יוֹתֵר³ כָּבוֹד דְּאַבָּא וְכָבוֹד דְּאִימָּא. וְעַל יְדֵי זֶה
הוּא יִחוּד אֲנַ״א [אַבָּא וְאִמָּא] וְיִחוּד זו״ן.

דְּעִם הֱיוֹת שֶׁשְּׁנֵיהֶם (כָּבוֹד (וְחוּפָּה) דְּאַנַ״א, וְכָבוֹד
(וְחוּפָּה) דְּזו״ן) הֵם בְּחִינַת מַקִּיף, מִכָּל מָקוֹם יָדוּעַ שֶׁדַּוְקָא
בְּיִחוּד זו״ן (שֶׁהוּא יִחוּד פְּנִימִי) נִמְשָׁךְ הָעֶצֶם.

---

order to understand a thing truly and profoundly as it evolves from the concept which he has conceived in his intellect, this is called *binah*. These [*chochmah* and *binah*] are the very "father" and "mother" which give birth to [the emotional faculties, such as] love of G-d, and awe and dread of Him."

In our text, the male and female aspects are likened to "groom and bride," and are matched with "*abba* and *imma*," lit., "father and mother"—"*chochmah* and *binah*," or, on a lower realm, "*z'a* and *nukva* (*malchut*)," as the discourse continues. In all of these levels there exists the *makif* of "honor," the "*chuppah*," which transcends and unifies them.

22. NUKVA. Literally, "female," this is another term for *malchut*. "Male" and "female" are terms used in Kabbalah to denote "giver" and "recipient," respectively. See above fn. 7, that *malchut* is a recipient from the *sefirot* above it, which is similar to a female, who is a recipient from the male giver.

To explain the concept of union: *Chochmah* in human terms refers to the highest level of the thinking process, the initial, unstructured flash of insight. At this stage, the person is still unable to explain the concept

even to himself. It is only at the next step, *binah*, that the seminal thought of *chochmah* is processed and developed, becoming firmly implanted in one's mind. Thus, *binah* serves as the receptacle for the insight of *chochmah*.

However, as explained in the previous footnote, for any practical result to ensue from *chochmah* and *binah*, i.e., for any "offspring" or *middot* (emotions) to be "born," there must be a union between them. This is only possible through a higher power, one that transcends both *chochmah* and *binah*. This is the meaning of the *chuppah*—a *makif*-type of light that encompasses *chochmah* and *binah*, unifying them into one.

On a lower scale, a similar union is brought about between *z'a* and *malchut*: They, too, are "giver" and "recipient" respectively, and become unified through a *chuppah*—a *makif*-type of light that encompasses and transcends both the six *middot* and the *sefirah* of *malchut*.

23. **Discourse entitled *Samach Tesamach, 5657*, p. 90 ff** [*Sefer Hamaamarim 5657*, p. 267], **et al. See also *Likkutei Torah*, ibid., 40a.**

24. The union of *z'a* and *malchut* is termed an "internal union" in com-

2.

FIRST EXAMPLE REVISITED

Now, the first example[25] is about the transmission from a
teacher to a student. The order of this is, as our Sages have related,[26] that before [Rabbah] would open to [begin teaching]
his students, he would make a humorous remark, which
would cause his students to laugh. After that, he would sit in
awe and open [i.e., begin] his teachings.[27]

HUMOROUS REMARK

This humorous remark [which may be categorized as the "casual conversation of Torah sages, which must be learned and
studied,"[28]] is considered merely an external representation of
the sage.[29] However, this transmission paves the way for the
internal transmission (of his teachings), for it is specifically
through this that the student's heart and mind will be opened
and receptive to the internal transmission.[30]

The story about Rabbah is first employed as an analogy
by Rabbi DovBer, second Lubavitcher Rebbe, in *Torat
Chaim*.[31]

[However, in *Torat Chaim* it is not cited as an analogy for

---

parison with that of *chochmah* and *binah*: A person's emotions are more internal than his intellect. When one
wishes to evaluate someone's personality, his "inner" self, one con-
siders his *character* and not so much
his academic level, for a person's behavior can be drastically different
than his intellectual degree. It is specifically the union of one's attributes
(*z'a* and *malchut*) that is called an "internal union;" furthermore, it is specifically in such a union that the person's essence (i.e., personality) is
revealed.

The two types of union—(a) intellect with reason, and (b) *z'a* with
malchut—are to be found in the
groom/bride relationship. The giving

of the ring by the groom is an internal union, for it is in itself quite profound and not solely peripheral. But
on the other hand, in relation to the
true, internal union, following the
wedding, from where offspring can be
born, the giving of the ring is only a
makif-type union (Hence the ring's
circular shape, symbolizing the "encompassing" *makif*.) (*Sefer Hamaamarim 5657*, pp. 270-1).

25. In Rabbi Yosef Yitzchak's discourse.

26. *Pesachim* 117a, where it is refer-
enced further.

27. Rabbah's method of teaching his

ב.

וְהִנֵּה הַמָּשָׁל הָרִאשׁוֹן הוּא מֵהַשְׁפָּעַת רַב לְתַלְמִיד, וְסֵדֶר הַהַשְׁפָּעָה הוּא כְּמוֹ שֶׁאָמְרוּ רַזַ״לְ׳ דְּמִקַּמֵּי דְּפָתַח לְהוּ לְרַבָּנָן אָמַר מִילְתָא דִּבְדִיחוּתָא וּבָדְחוּ רַבָּנָן וּלְבַסוֹף יָתִיב בְּאֵימְתָא וּפָתַח בִּשְׁמַעְתָּא,

דְּהַמִּילְתָא דִּבְדִיחוּתָא שֶׁקּוֹדֶם הַלִּימוּד [שֶׁהוּא עִנְיַן שִׂיחַת חוּלִּין שֶׁל תַּלְמִידֵי חֲכָמִים שֶׁצְּרִיכָה לִימוּד׳׳] הִיא חִיצוֹנִית בִּלְבָד, אָמְנָם הַשְׁפָּעָה זוֹ הִיא הַקְדָּמָה לְהַהַשְׁפָּעָה פְּנִימִית (דְּפָתַח בִּשְׁמַעְתָּא) כִּי דַּוְקָא עַל יְדֵי זֶה נַעֲשָׂה פְּתִיחַת הַלֵּב וְהַמּוֹחַ שֶׁל הַתַּלְמִיד שֶׁיִּהְיֶה כְּלִי לְקַבָּלָה לְהַהַשְׁפָּעָה פְּנִימִית.

וְהִנֵּה מְקוֹר מָשָׁל זֶה הוּא מֵאַדְמוֹ״ר הָאֶמְצָעִי בְּתוֹרַת חַיִּים״,

[אֶלָּא שֶׁבְּתוֹרַת חַיִּים זֶה הוּבָא לֹא כְּמָשָׁל לְהָעִנְיָן דִּלְכָה

---

students demonstrates the process required for any transmission from giver to receiver to take place, as the discourse proceeds to explain.

28. *Sukkah* 21b; *Avodah Zarah* 19b. See *Rashi* on *Sukkah*, ibid.: "One must listen attentively even to the casual conversation of the Sages, for from these words Torah thoughts can be derived.... One must listen to them and take them to heart." *Rashi* on *Avodah Zarah*, ibid., comments: "One ought to [even] listen to the casual conversation of the Sages so that he may learn how to speak in the *manner* of the Sages, whose words are pure, rich, and offer healing."

29. Although there is much to be learned from even the casual conversation of Torah sages, these sayings

in no way represent the true depth and brilliance of the sage.

In Chasidus, the deep, brilliant thoughts of the Torah sage are referred to as his "inner" dimension (*penimiyut*), as they reflect his true and inner brilliance. His humorous remarks (and casual conversation), conversely, are referred to as merely his "external" dimension (*chitzoniyut*), as they do not capture his true and inner brilliance.

30. This demonstrates that any deep, internal transmission from giver to receiver must be preceded by an external transmission that establishes a preliminary, basic connection between them.

31. In the discourse entitled *V'eleh Toldot*, Chapter 6 (2d).

the concept of *Lecha Dodi*. In the discourse entitled *Semuchim La'ad*, 5680[32] (the discourse delivered by Rabbi Shalom Dov-Ber, fifth Lubavitcher Rebbe, on the occasion of his final birthday (20 Marcheshvan) in this world) it says that "*perhaps*" there is a connection between the concept of Rabbah's humorous remark and that of *Lecha Dodi*. But in *Lecha Dodi*, 5689, my father-in-law, the Rebbe, omitted the word "perhaps" and wrote it as obvious.[33]]

PURE PLEASURE

Torat Chaim continues (thereafter[34]) that the root of laughter is [the soul's] pure indivisible pleasure.[35]

From this we infer that the root of the humorous remark (which is pure pleasure) is higher than the transmission of the subsequent teachings (for intellectual pleasure is a composite pleasure).[36]

However, this [the humorous remark] is only external, and it is through the internal transmission that one can reach an even loftier realm.[37]

---

32. Chapter 1 (published in booklet form by Kehot, 1952). [It was subsequently printed in *Sefer Hamaamarim 5680*, p. 148.]

33. The following incident is also well known: On one occasion, when Rabbi Shalom DovBer delivered a discourse in private before his son—my father-in-law, the Rebbe— he mentioned a topic (about an example for the faculty of imagination) suggesting it as probable. Later on, when my father-in-law, the Rebbe, visited his father-in-law, Rabbi Avraham [Schneersohn] in Kishinev, the latter requested that he recite a Chasidic discourse, remarking, "Just open up the faucet and it will come pouring out!" My father-in-law, the Rebbe, then proceeded to recite the very discourse that he had heard from

his father in private, along with the example, but stating that it was obvious. When he returned to Lubavitch, he related the incident to his father, Rabbi Shalom DovBer, who asked, "Where did you get that from [that it's obvious]? I only said it was *probable*." My father-in-law, the Rebbe, answered, "What is probable to you is obvious to me."

34. Chapter 12 (5c).

35. There are two types of pleasure: 1) A composite pleasure that is garbed in an external factor, so that there is a combination of two aspects, the pleasure and the subject of the pleasure. In Hebrew, this is called *taanug hamurkav*; 2) An indivisible, pure pleasure. In Hebrew, this is called *taanug hapashut shebilti murkav*

דּוֹדִי. וּבְדָרוּשׁ הַמַּתְחִיל סְמוּכִים לָעַד פר״ת׳ (הַמַּאֲמָר שֶׁאָמַר כְּבוֹד קְדֻשַּׁת אַדְמוּ״ר מְהוֹרָש״ב נִשְׁמָתוֹ עֵדֶן בְּיוֹם הוֹלַדְתּוֹ (כ׳ מַרְחֶשְׁוָן) הָאַחֲרוֹן בְּעָלְמָא דֵין) מְקֻשָּׁר בְּדֶרֶךְ אֶפְשָׁר ("וְאֶפְשָׁר שֶׁזֶּה עִנְיַן כו׳") הָעִנְיָן דְּמִילְתָא דִּבְדִיחוּתָא לְהָעִנְיָן דְּלָכָה דוֹדִי. וּבְדָרוּשׁ הַמַּתְחִיל לְכָה דוֹדִי הִשְׁמִיט כְּבוֹד קְדֻשַּׁת מוֹרִי וְחָמִי אַדְמוּ״ר תֵּיבַת "וְאֶפְשָׁר" וְכוֹתֵב זֶה בִּפְשִׁיטוּת[יא],

וּבְתוֹרַת חַיִּים שָׁם (לְאַחַר זֶה[יב]) מְבָאֵר, דְּשֹׁרֶשׁ עִנְיַן הַשְּׂחוֹק הוּא מִתַּעֲנוּג הַפָּשׁוּט שֶׁבְּלִתִּי מוּרְכָּב כְּלָל.

וּמִזֶּה מוּבָן, דְּשֹׁרֶשׁ שֶׁל מִילְתָא דִּבְדִיחוּתָא (שֶׁהוּא תַּעֲנוּג הַפָּשׁוּט) הוּא לְמַעְלָה מֵהַשְׁפָּעַת הַשֵּׂכֶל שֶׁלְּאַחַר זֶה (שֶׁהֲרֵי הַתַּעֲנוּג שֶׁבַּשֵּׂכֶל הוּא תַּעֲנוּג מוּרְכָּב).

אָמְנָם מִכָּל מָקוֹם הֲרֵי זֶה רַק בְּחִינַת חִיצוֹנִית, וְעַל יְדֵי הַהַשְׁפָּעָה פְּנִימִית מַגִּיעִים לְעִילּוּי נַעֲלֶה יוֹתֵר.

---

klal. This is the *capability* that the soul possesses to garner pleasure from any given factor—i.e., this is the *essence of the faculty* of pleasure, not the actual pleasure gained from any external factor.

Torat Chaim explains that the purpose of the humorous remark is to awaken the faculty of pleasure in the student. Besides enjoying the sharp-witted humor, which would be categorized as the first of the two aforementioned types of pleasure, the student's actual faculty of pleasure becomes awakened. As a result, the student is in a state of delight, and his mental faculties are opened. He is then able to receive and understand the teacher's lesson.

36. I.e., the pleasure derived from in-

tellect is not an expression of the soul's capability for pleasure; rather, it is pleasure that was *caused* by intellect. In other words, it is only a *result* of the intellect, and is not an expression of the essence of the soul's inherent faculty of pleasure.

The humorous remark, on the other hand, awakens the essence of the faculty of pleasure as it exists within the soul, and hence is of a higher root.

37. After all, as explained above in the main text, the humorous remark is considered to be merely an external representation (*chitzoniyut*) of the teacher. See also above, fn. 29, that the humorous remark of the teacher in no way represents his true depth and brilliance. His genius is found ex-

TWO "PURE PLEASURES"

To explain: There are two levels of pure pleasure[38]—one that can be felt, and one that cannot be felt; an "essence-type" of pleasure.[39] But through internal transmission specifically [i.e., actual teachings], where the student receives internally, the essence-type of pleasure that cannot be felt is, in fact, attainable.[40] Thus, our Sages said, "From my students I learned more than from all the others."[41]

3.

SECOND EXAMPLE REVISITED

The second example is about a father who wishes to play with his very young son face-to-face. Since the child is small, the

---

clusively in his teachings, termed in Chasidus as the teacher's "inner" dimension (*penimiyut*), for they reflect his true and inner brilliance.

And the student, by concentrating on the teacher's actual teachings—the *internal* transmission from the teacher—rather than on the humorous remark, will rise to true heights. Hence, although the humorous remark was necessary to open his senses, and has a loftier root (that of "pure pleasure"), it is by no means the greatest level, for it acts as an "external," not internal, transmission.

38. *Yom Tov Shel Rosh Hashanah 5666*, p. 99 ff; *V'haya ki tavo, 5675* (in *B'Shaah Shehikdimu 5672*, vol. 2 [p. 1123 ff]).

39. There are two levels within the category of "pure pleasure": 1) How the pleasure becomes awakened and revealed. This is known as "pure pleasure that can be felt" (in Hebrew—*taanug hapashut hamurgash*); 2) The essence of the pleasure that

cannot be revealed or discerned at all. This is known as "essence-type pure pleasure that cannot be felt" (in Hebrew—*taanug ha'atzmi habilti murgash*).

For example, some things within one's mind and heart one feels and is aware of, and other things are so deeply engraved within the soul, and are so concealed, that the person is not even aware of them himself. These things function in a hidden way, such as when a person feels compelled to do something, but doesn't know why or what forced him.

The same applies to pleasure. There is a faculty of pleasure so deep within the essence of the soul that it cannot be felt or discerned. For example, when a person becomes completely taken and overwhelmed by sheer pleasure that he remains "rooted to the spot" and cannot express his feelings in any form whatsoever.

40. The humorous remark awakens the level of "pure pleasure that can be felt." But through internal trans-

וְהָעִנְיָן הוּא דִּבְתַעֲנוּג הַפָּשׁוּט גּוּפָא יֵשׁ בּ׳ דַּרְגוֹת, [41]
תַּעֲנוּג הַפָּשׁוּט הַמּוּרְגָּשׁ וְתַעֲנוּג הָעַצְמִי הַבִּלְתִּי מוּרְגָּשׁ.
וְדַוְקָא עַל יְדֵי הַהַשְׁפָּעָה פְּנִימִית, שֶׁהַתַּלְמִיד מְקַבֵּל
בִּפְנִימִיּוּתוֹ, מַגִּיעִים לְתַעֲנוּג הָעַצְמִי הַבִּלְתִּי מוּרְגָּשׁ. וְלָכֵן
אָמְרוּ רַזַ"ל וּמִתַּלְמִידַי יוֹתֵר מִכּוּלָן.

ג.

וּמָשָׁל הַב׳ הוּא מִבֵּן יָנִיק וְקָטָן שֶׁאָבִיו רוֹצֶה לְהִשְׁתַּעֲשֵׁעַ
עִמּוֹ פָּנִים אֶל פָּנִים וַהֲרֵי הַתִּינוֹק הוּא קָטָן, צָרִיךְ הָאָב

---

mission, although it comes after the teacher measures his words so that his lesson is not too advanced for his students, the teacher attains the level of "essence-type pure pleasure that cannot be felt"—for he derives so much pleasure from teaching that it touches his essence. See note below.

41. *Taanit* 7a. See below, Chapter 7. The Talmud states: "R. Chanina said, 'I have learned much from my teachers. I learned more from my friends than from my teachers. But from my students I learned more than from all the others.'"

Chasidus explains that a teacher derives immense pleasure from teaching, for "absolute pleasure in having transmitted a lesson is possible only when the teacher sees that the student properly grasped the subject matter... for that is the purpose of his teaching" (*B'Shaah Shehikdimu 5672*, vol. 2, p. 1120. See also *Torat Chaim, Vayigash* 89d ff). This implies that the student's grasping of the transmission is more valuable to the teacher than the actual transmission, and there-

fore, affects the teacher in a much more profound way.

So the three levels of pleasure discussed here as they relate to the teacher-student scenario are: 1) A pleasure combined of external factors—taking pleasure in the intellectual subject; 2) Pure pleasure that can be felt—the student enjoying the introductory humorous remark; 3) Essence-type pure pleasure that cannot be felt—the teacher deriving pleasure from the fact that the student understood and grasped the lesson.

* * *

To apply the example in this chapter to the subject at hand: There is an initial, external transmission from teacher to student—the humorous remark. This paves the way for the subsequent internal transmission—the actual lesson. But by teaching the students, the teacher gains immensely, rising "ever higher" in knowledge and pleasure—as the sage who said, "From my students I learned more than from all the others." The teacher enjoys a level of pleasure unattainable had he not taught.

father must lower his hands [which are normally above the child's head, until they are underneath the child] to pick up his young son, so that he can play with him up close, face-to-face. Picking up the child is a completely external action, and is only a prelude to the internal connection that follows (the amusement, etc.).[42]

SPIRITUAL GAMES

This story is first employed as an analogy by Rabbi DovBer, the Maggid of Mezritch, in *Or Torah*,[43] where there is an additional point (not cited in the discourse [by my father-in-law, the Rebbe][44]): the young son "plays with his (father's) beard."

This [playing] alludes to the fact that the transmission of the *makif* (prior to the internal transmission[45]) transcends *hishtalshelut*.[46] For a beard corresponds to the Thirteen Garments of the Beard—the Thirteen Attributes of Mercy[47] that transcend *hishtalshelut*.[48] Nevertheless, there does exist some sense of relationship between them and *hishtalshelut*, as the verse says, *Remember Your mercies... for they are related to the*

---

42. In this example, the "internal transmission" is the father's playing with his son, as this is what makes the child happy. Picking up the child is (relative to their playing) merely an "external" act for both father and child. For the father: picking up his son is a very limited interaction, one that does not *openly* express his love for his child (as playing does). For the child: the child does not (necessarily) sense his father's love in the act of picking up; the child merely sees that he or she is being brought closer to the father (and may not even realize that it is the father that is picking him or her up). Only later, when they actually play together, does the child feel the father's love.

43. **85d** [on the verse *I sent to Efraim*

and took them upon My arms (Hosea 11:3)].

44. Nor is it cited in *Likkutei Torah, Pinchas* 80b; *Semuchim La'ad*, ibid.

45. Generally, the amusement corresponds to the idea of internal connection (as mentioned above, quoting *Lecha Dodi, 5689*). However, compared to any academics and inner transmission that a son may receive from his father, and the like, amusement is also a form of external connection.

46. HISHTALSHELUT. "Progression," or, in its full name, *seder hishtalshelut*—the order or chain of worlds—means the giving of life to the various levels of creation through

לְהַשְׁפִּיל אֶת יָדָיו כו׳ לְהָרִים בְּנוֹ הַקָטָן בִּכְדֵי שֶׁיּוּכַל לְהִשְׁתַּעֲשֵׁעַ עִמּוֹ בְּקֵירוּב פָּנִים אֶל פָּנִים. דְּהַגְבָּהַת הַתִּינוֹק הוּא רַק עִנְיָן חִיצוֹנִי, וְהוּא רַק הַקְדָּמָה לְהַקֵירוּב פְּנִימִי שֶׁלְּאַחַר זֶה (הַשַּׁעֲשׁוּעִים כו׳).

וְהִנֵּה מְקוֹר מָשָׁל זֶה הוּא בְּאוֹר תּוֹרָה לְהָרַב הַמַּגִּידטּ, וְשָׁם יֶשְׁנָה הוֹסָפָה (שֶׁלֹּא נֶעְתְּקָה בְּהַמַּאֲמַרטּ), שֶׁהַקָטָן "מִשְׁתַּעֲשֵׁעַ בִּזְקַן שֶׁלּוֹ" (שֶׁל הָאָב).

וְיֵשׁ לוֹמַר שֶׁבְּזֶה מְרוּמָז, שֶׁהַמַּשְׁכַת הַמַּקִּיף (שֶׁקּוֹדֶם הַהַשְׁפָּעָה פְּנִימִיתט) הִיא לְמַעְלָה מֵהִשְׁתַּלְשְׁלוּת, דְּזָקָן הוּא י״ג תִּיקּוּנֵי דִיקְנָא, י״ג מִדּוֹת הָרַחֲמִים שֶׁלְּמַעְלָה מֵהִשְׁתַּלְשְׁלוּת. אֶלָּא מִכָּל מָקוֹם יֵשׁ לָהֶם אֵיזוֹ שַׁיָּיכוּת לְהִשְׁתַּלְשְׁלוּת, כְּמוֹ שֶׁנֶּאֱמַרטּ זְכוֹר רַחֲמֶיךָ גו׳ כִּי מֵעוֹלָם הֵמָּה [שֶׁלָּכֵן

---

a process of gradual and ordered descent and downward gradation, by means of numerous contractions of the divine force.

47. THIRTEEN ATTRIBUTES OF MERCY. *L-rd, L-rd, benevolent G-d, compassionate and gracious, slow to anger and abounding in kindness and truth; He preserves kindness for two thousand generations, forgiving iniquity, transgression and sin, and He cleanses* (Exodus 34:6-7). G-d wrapped Himself as the one who leads the prayers and showed Moshe the order of the prayer. G-d said, "When the Jewish people sin, they are to perform this order before Me, and I shall forgive them." Said R. Yehudah: A covenant was made for the Thirteen Attributes that they will not be returned empty-handed, as it says (Exodus 34:10), *I hereby make a covenant* (*Rosh Hashanah* 17b).

Kabbalistic works term these Thirteen Attributes the "Thirteen Garments of the [Supernal] Beard." The beard only begins to grow when one reaches adulthood and one's intellect matures. At this point, one becomes a vessel for that which transcends intellect, which parallels *hishtalshelut*. When the child plays with the beard, he elicits from that lofty realm that transcends "matured intellect"—the Essence-type love of father for his child.

Hence the correlation of the beard to the Thirteen Attributes of Mercy, both of which transcend *hishtalshelut*.

48. Since the Thirteen Attributes transcend *hishtalshelut*, and hence, all of worlds, which are limited in some way, they are therefore "boundless mercy," and "will not be returned empty-handed," as cited above from the Talmud.

worlds.[49] [This is why the attributes are called *middot* in Hebrew, a word that is etymologically related to *medidah* (measure)[50]]. In addition, it is known that "hairs" are merely a ray.[51]

ELICITING ESSENCE

However, through the subsequent internal transmission (although of lesser quality than the *makif*), the essence, which transcends the *makif*, is elicited. (This is similar to the discussion above in Chapter 1 regarding the advantage of the union of *z'a* and *malchut* (which is an internal union) over the union of *abba* and *imma*—as the Tzemach Tzedek explained on a number of occasions.[52])

4.

A similar concept exists in *avodah*[53] (as the discourse [of my

---

49. Psalms 25:6. See also the discourse entitled *Asher Bara, 5689*, Ch. 3 (23a in the booklet of *Derushei Chatunah* [*Sefer Hamaamarim 5689*, p. 89]). Chasidus infers from this verse that there *does* exist *some* relationship between the Attributes of Mercy and *hishtalshelut*. For "attribute" in Hebrew is *middah*, from the word *medidah* (measure), and the *hishtalshelut* is a process of gradation and contraction, read: limitation.

(Although the verse literally means that G-d's mercy and kindness have existed since the start of creation (see *Rashi*, ad loc), here the verse is translated in a Chasidic light: the Hebrew word *mei'olam* is understood to mean *from the world*. I.e., G-d's mercy and kindness are *related to the world*, for the concepts of mercy and kindness come into play specifically after creation, when the concept of *hishtalshelut* exists. See *Torat Shmuel—Sefer 5633*, vol. 2, p. 541 and fn. there.)

50. *Or Hatorah, Vayera* 93b; *Yom Tov Shel Rosh Hashanah 5666*, p. 285.

51. The fact that the Thirteen Attributes are called "beard," i.e., "hair," denotes that they are merely a manifestation of G-d, and not His very Essence. This further underlines the limitation of these Attributes in relation to G-d's Essence. The analogy from hair is that although the hair on one's head lives from the brain, the vitality in hair is so minute that one feels no pain when the hair is cut—in contrast to any of the body's limbs, which contains the life-force of the soul within it and sense pain when cut.

(In the example above, when the child plays with his father's beard, he is not reaching the father's essence at that stage. Only later on, when the child receives some internal transmission from his father, does he receive of his father's essence.)

נִקְרָאוֹת בְּשֵׁם "מִדּוֹת" מִלְּשׁוֹן מְדִידָה["]. גַּם יָדוּעַ בְּעִנְיַן
הַשַּׁעֲרוֹת שֶׁהוּא הֶאָרָה בִּלְבָד.

אָמְנָם עַל יְדֵי הַהַשְׁפָּעָה פְּנִימִית שֶׁלְּאַחַר זֶה (אַף שֶׁהִיא
לְמַטָּה מִבְּחִינַת מַקִּיף) נִמְשָׁךְ הָעֶצֶם שֶׁלְּמַעְלָה מֵהַמַּקִּיף (עַל
דֶּרֶךְ הַנַּ"ל [הַנִּזְכָּר לְעֵיל] סְעִיף א' בְּמַעֲלַת יְחוּד זוּ"ן (שֶׁהוּא
יְחוּד פְּנִימִי) עַל יְחוּד אַנְ"א כְּבֵיאוּר אַדְמוּ"ר הַצֶּמַח צֶדֶק
בְּכַמָּה מְקוֹמוֹת[ ] בָּזֶה).

ד.

וְעַל דֶּרֶךְ זֶה הוּא בַּעֲבוֹדָה (כְּמוֹ שֶׁמְּבֹאָר בְּהַמַּאֲמָר[ ]),

---

52. **See the index of the Tzemach Tzedek's works.** From *Derech Mitzvotecha*, 3a ff; *Biurei Hazohar*, vol. 2, p. 612 ff: A teacher can only transmit to a student if the latter possesses the capability to understand, but he can never create a mind for the student. However, a physical union can produce a child with qualities superior to his parents'! Wouldn't the opposite be true—that the high value of intellect could change the recipient's intellectual powers? The answer is that intellect, though powerful, is merely a ray from the soul, and not its essence. Consequently, it is useful only to one who already has the means to receive it; it cannot *create* a recipient. In a physical union, however, the *essence* comes into play, and this can give birth to a complete child, who can even possess even greater talents than his parents.

In spiritual terms, it is the union of *z'a* and *malchut* that gives birth to something of essence, as opposed to the union of *abba* and *imma*, which only can produce something in-

tellectual. See above, fn. 24.

* * *

To apply the example in this chapter to the subject at hand: The initial, external transmission from father to son occurs when the father picks up the son. This paves the way for the subsequent internal transmission—the father playing with the son. This transmission elicits to the son the father's essence, i.e., his inner, deep love for the son.

53. AVODAH. Lit., "service"; "divine service." In Chabad philosophy, *avodah* also implies effort.

The root of the word *avodah* (עבודה) comprises the letters *ayin, bet, dalet*. The same root is used to describe the tanning of a hide (*orot avudin*—"tanned hides"). The hide is not suitable for use as is; it becomes usable leather only after a thorough processing. Likewise, the animal soul within a person becomes fit to serve G-d only through the hard work of transforming it, as explained below in fn. 70. The person must do this work

father-in-law] explains[54]). Every day, a person's spiritual service begins with prayer, as the verse says, *Withdraw from man
who has the soul in his nostrils, for with what* (bameh) *is he
deemed [worthy]?*[55] [Our Sages commented on this verse] "Do
not read the word as *bameh* ('with what'), but rather as *bamah*
('a platform')."[56]

Rabbi Schneur Zalman of Liadi and Rabbi Shmuel,
fourth Lubavitcher Rebbe, explain[57] that before one prays,
one is deemed a *bamah*, a platform.[58]

PRAYER

"Prayer" means "connection,"[59] for through prayer one connects with G-d. The order of the prayers is that there must
first be a general connection (an external transmission) [as explained in the discourse[60]], and only then can the internal
transmission take place. I.e., the person connects himself to
G-dliness to the extent that he draws G-dliness into all his
physical matters.[61]

---

himself; there is no automatic inspiration, as there is for the G-dly
soul (*Transforming the Inner Self* (Kehot, 2004), fn. 85).

The term "service" (*avodah*), applies only to what a person does with
immense exertion, contrary to his
soul's inclination (*Iggeret Hakodesh*,
12 (*Tanya* 118a-b. Bi-Lingual Edition, pp. 453-5)).

Avodah in the Chasidic lexicon
refers to the refinement and improve-
ment of character traits, and a deep-
rooted inward attachment to G-d
(*Hayom Yom*, 6 Tevet).

54. **Chapter 3.**

55. Isaiah 2:22.

56. *Berachot* 14a.

57. *Likkutei Torah, Pinchas* 79d; In-

troduction to *Likkutei Torah L'Gimmel Parshiyot* by Rabbi Shmuel of
Lubavitch. [This is printed in *Or Hatorah, Bereshit*, vol. 6, p. 1020a.]

58. One who has yet to connect with
G-dliness (through prayer) senses his
own being and existence, the "I."
That is why before a person prays
(when his soul does not yet radiate
throughout his body) he is considered
a *bamah* (platform), a term that implies haughtiness and independence.

59. The Hebrew word for prayer is *tefillah*. The etymological root of *tefillah* (תפילה) is *tafal* (תפל), which
means to "paste" or "bind." (See *Torah Or, Terumah* 79d, et al. See also
Torat Menachem—Hitvaaduyot 5712,
vol. 7, p. 17, fn. 8.) In a deeper sense,
then, the "service of prayer" (*tefillah*)
entails toiling (during prayer) to *bind*

שֶׁהַתְחָלַת עֲבוֹדַת הָאָדָם בְּכָל יוֹם הִיא עֲבוֹדַת הַתְּפִלָּה,
כְּמוֹ שֶׁנֶּאֱמַר[כב] חִדְלוּ לָכֶם מִן הָאָדָם אֲשֶׁר נִשְׁמָה בְּאַפּוֹ כִּי
בַמֶּה נֶחְשָׁב הוּא, אַל תִּקְרֵי בַּמֶּה אֶלָּא בָמֶה[כג],

וּבֵיאֲרוּ אַדְמוֹ"ר הַזָּקֵן וְאַדְמוֹ"ר מַהֲרַ"שׁ[כד] דְּקוֹדֶם הַתְּפִלָּה
נֶחְשָׁב הָאָדָם כְּמוֹ בָמָה.

וּתְפִלָּה הוּא לְשׁוֹן הִתְחַבְּרוּת[כה], שֶׁעַל יְדֵי הַתְּפִלָּה
מִתְקַשֵּׁר הָאָדָם בֵּאלֹקוּת. וְסֵדֶר הַתְּפִלָּה הוּא, שֶׁמְּקוּדָם
צָרִיךְ לִהְיוֹת הַקֵּירוּב כְּלָלִי (הַמְשָׁכָה חִיצוֹנִית) [כְּמוֹ
שֶׁמְּבֹאָר עִנְיָנוּ בְּהַמַּאֲמָר[כא]], וְאַחַר כַּךְ נַעֲשֶׂה הַקֵּירוּב פְּנִימִי,
שֶׁהָאָדָם מִתְקַשֵּׁר לֵאלֹקוּת בְּאוֹפֶן כָּזֶה שֶׁמַּמְשִׁיךְ אֱלֹקוּת
בְּכָל עִנְיָנָיו הַגַּשְׁמִיִּים.

---

and *connect* oneself with G-d.

60. From *Lecha Dodi, 5689*: "Now, in order for this deep, internal connection [between G-d and man] to occur, to the extent that one even elicits G-dliness within all his physical matters, there must first be a more general [external] connection. This is why our Sages say (*Berachot* 5:1) that "only with a sense of earnestness may one begin to pray"—which *Rashi* (*Berachot* 30b, s.v. *koved rosh*) explains as referring to the quality of surrender and humility, for this establishes the initial, general connection [between man and G-d]."

Before a person can attain an "internal" connection with G-dliness—a state in which he is so connected with G-dliness that his soul's radiance permeates his entire being—he must first establish a basic "external" connection with G-dliness.

That is why our Sages said that before prayer one must awaken within himself feelings of surrender and humility, as this represents one's most *basic* approach to G-dliness: one accepts upon himself, before he begins his "service of the heart" (prayer), to completely surrender himself to G-dliness. Only afterwards can he commence his prayers, and begin to feel G-dliness "internally."

61. When the holiness of the soul is felt within even the coarse physical body, then all of one's mundane *actions* will similarly be permeated with a holy purpose. One will eat and drink not to satisfy his base cravings, but rather to energize himself so that he may study more Torah and fulfill *mitzvot*; one will involve himself in business matters not for greedy purposes, but rather so that he will be able to assist those less fortunate than him.

So it is prayer that grants one the power to transform all his physical affairs into conduits for G-dliness, to

HONORING ONE'S OLDEST BROTHER

To understand [how beginning the day with prayer enables one to connect and transform all his physical matters into conduits for G-dliness]:

The Baal Shem Tov explained[62] the prohibition of exchanging a greeting before prayer[63] by comparing it to what is written in the Arizal's Writings[64] regarding honoring one's oldest brother.[65] The father's spirit resides more in the oldest son than in the later sons, who all obtain their father's spirit through the oldest son. In turn, due to this spirit residing more in the oldest brother, they are obligated to honor him as they are obligated to honor their father. [This explains why the law pertaining to honoring the oldest brother is derived from the verse, *Honor your father*,[66] for honoring one's oldest brother is contained within honoring one's father.]

FIRST MORNING STATEMENT

The same is true [explains the Baal Shem Tov] regarding one's thought, speech, and deeds throughout the day—they all branch off and are drawn from the first statement (in the morning).[67] Thus, one's first statement [and likewise, thoughts and deeds] upon arising from sleep ought to be in the service of G-d. In this manner, one elicits holiness into all his thoughts, speech, and deeds throughout the entire day.[68]

It is specifically through the person's internal connection to G-dliness (during prayer), in a manner that draws G-dliness into all his physical matters to the extent of transforming them into conduits for G-dliness, that one can reach

---

serve G-d even with physical matters. As mentioned, the preparation for this is the general connection, the external transmission—the surrender and humility before G-d.

62. *Keter Shem Tov* (Kehot), #212.

63. *Berachot* ibid. *Tur* and *Shulchan*

Aruch (and *Shulchan Aruch Harav*), *Orach Chaim*, 89:2 (3).

64. *Shaar Hamitzvot, Yitro; Likkutei Torah, Vayera.* See *Zohar* III:83a.

65. *Ketubot* 103a.

66. Exodus 20:12.

וְיוּבַן זֶה [מַה שֶּׁעַל יְדֵי הַתְּפִלָּה בִּתְחִלַּת הַיּוֹם בִּיכָלְתּוֹ
לְקַשֵּׁר כָּל הָעִנְיָנִים הַגַּשְׁמִיִּים וְלַעֲשׂוֹתָם כֵּלִים לֶאֱלֹקוּת]:

עַל פִּי מַה שֶּׁבֵּיאֵר הַבַּעַל שֵׁם טוֹב^{טו} עִנְיַן אִיסוּר שְׁאִילַת
שָׁלוֹם קוֹדֶם הַתְּפִלָּה^{טז}, שֶׁהוּא עַל דֶּרֶךְ מַה שֶּׁכָּתוּב בְּכִתְבֵי
הָאֲרִיזַ"ל^{יז} בְּעִנְיַן כִּיבּוּד אָח הַגָּדוֹל^{יח}, שֶׁהוּא מִפְּנֵי דְרוּחָא
הוּא דְשָׁבַק בְּגַוֵּיהּ, שֶׁבֵּבֶן הָא' יֵשׁ רוּחַ הָאָב יוֹתֵר מִשְּׁאָר
הַבָּנִים, וְכָל שְׁאָר הַבָּנִים נוֹטְלִים מֵרוּחָא דְאָב עַל יְדֵי בֵּן
הָרִאשׁוֹן. וּמִצַּד רוּחַ הָאָב שֶׁבָּאָח הַגָּדוֹל מְחוּיָּיבִים הֵם
לְכַבְּדוֹ כְּמוֹ שֶׁהֵם מְחוּיָּיבִים בִּכְבוֹד הָאָב [שֶׁלָּכֵן לְמֵדִין^{יט} דִּין
זֶה מֵהַפָּסוּק^ל כַּבֵּד אֶת אָבִיךָ דַּוְקָא, כִּי כְּבוֹד אָח הַגָּדוֹל נִכְלָל
בִּכְיבּוּד אָב].

וּכְמוֹ כֵן הוּא בְּנוֹגֵעַ לְמַחֲשָׁבָה דִּבּוּר וּמַעֲשֶׂה שֶׁל הָאָדָם
בְּמֶשֶׁךְ כָּל הַיּוֹם, שֶׁכּוּלָם מִסְתַּעֲפִין וְנִמְשָׁכִין אַחַר הַדִּבּוּר
הָרִאשׁוֹן, וְלָכֵן דִּבּוּר [וְכֵן מַחֲשָׁבָה וּמַעֲשֶׂה] הָרִאשׁוֹן שֶׁל
הָאָדָם בְּקוּמוֹ מִשְּׁינָתוֹ צָרִיךְ לִהְיוֹת בַּעֲבוֹדַת ה', שֶׁעַל יְדֵי
זֶה מַמְשִׁיךְ קְדוּשָׁה בְּכָל הַמַּחֲשָׁבָה דִּבּוּר וּמַעֲשֶׂה שֶׁלּוֹ בְּמֶשֶׁךְ
כָּל הַיּוֹם כּוּלּוֹ.

וְהִנֵּה דַּוְקָא עַל יְדֵי זֶה שֶׁהַקֵּירוּב פְּנִימִי שֶׁלּוֹ לֶאֱלֹקוּת
(בְּעֵת הַתְּפִלָּה) הוּא בְּאוֹפֶן כָּזֶה שֶׁמַּמְשִׁיךְ אוֹר אֱלֹקִי
בְּעִנְיָנָיו הַגַּשְׁמִיִּים עַד שֶׁעוֹשֶׂה אוֹתָם כֵּלִים לֶאֱלֹקוּת

---

67. The *Modeh Ani*, recited immedi-
ately upon awaking, in which one ac-
knowledges G-d as the "everlasting
King" (see *Siddur Tehillat Hashem*,
beg.).

68. Although the first statement uttered in the morning is indeed a holy
one, recited "in the service of G-d," it
is only of the *makif*-type, for at that
moment the person has not yet en-
gaged in the full service of prayer.

The body's strength has fully renewed
itself after a night of rest, making it
thus difficult for the soul to fully express itself within the body. Rather,
only a small "glimmer" of the soul's
radiance manifests itself.

It is only subsequently, during
prayer, that one is able to become internally connected to G-d to the
extent that all one's physical affairs
are transformed into conduits for
G-dliness.

ever higher—as is known[69] regarding, *Many crops come through the strength of an ox.*[70]

5.

FROM Z'A TO MALCHUT

In a similar vein, we can comprehend the transmission from *z'a* into *malchut* (in other words, "the union of *z'a* and *nukva*").[71]

The order of the transmission is thus (as explained above, Chapter 1): First there must be an external transmission, and then an internal transmission. The external transmission is indeed of extremely lofty caliber (similar to the explanations provided above, Chapters 2 and 3), for it is of the category of *makif*, which transcends *hishtalshelut* and *keilim*.[72] (The external transmission is therefore not integrated internally within *malchut*, for it is more sublime than *malchut's* limitations.)

However, this transmission is an external one, for it is merely a ray. In contrast, with an internal transmission, which

---

69. See *Likkutei Torah, Haazinu* 75b, et al.

70. **Proverbs 14:4.** The purpose of man possessing an animal soul is in order to harness its power for holy purposes, by transforming all of his physical affairs into conduits for G-dliness. This is accomplished by serving G-d even with physical objects at his disposal—by utilizing them for sacred purposes, such as *mitzvot.* The great animal-power enjoyed by the animal soul, the "ox," then serves as an extra boost of strength to the G-dly soul, when directed by the latter in serving G-d. The person who accomplishes this rises "ever higher" to an elevated level, a level otherwise unattainable merely with the G-dly soul.

* * *

This chapter has also demonstrated the three stages of external and internal transmission and the revelation of essence: The first statement in the morning, the *Modeh Ani*, establishes an external connection between a person and G-d. This then paves the way for a deeper, internal connection during prayer. Finally, by drawing G-d into all one's physical matters to the extent of transforming them into conduits of G-dliness, one provides an extra boost of strength to the G-dly soul, enabling it to reach "ever higher" than before.

71. In the preceding chapters, the discourse elaborated on the examples cited by Rabbi Yosef Yitzchak in his discourse of *Lecha Dodi* to illustrate the advantage of external transmission, and conversely, how the internal trans-

מַגִּיעִים לְמַעְלָה יוֹתֵר, כְּיָדוּעַᵃᵃ בְּעִנְיַן וְרַבⁱᵇ תְּבוּאוֹת בְּכֹחַ שׁוֹר.

ה.

וּכְמוֹ כֵן יוּבַן גַּם בְּעִנְיַן הַמְשָׁכַת הַזָּ״א בְּמַלְכוּת (יִחוּד זוּ״ן),

שֶׁהַסֵּדֶר בָּזֶה הוּא (כַּנַּ״ל סָעִיף א׳) אֲשֶׁר מִקּוֹדֶם צְרִיכָה לִהְיוֹת הַהַמְשָׁכָה חִיצוֹנִית וְאַחַר כַּךְ הַהַמְשָׁכָה פְּנִימִית. דְּגַם הַהַמְשָׁכָה חִיצוֹנִית הִיא הַמְשָׁכָה נַעֲלֵית בְּיוֹתֵר (עַל דֶּרֶךְ הַנַּ״ל סָעִיף ב-ג׳, שֶׁהִיא בְּחִינַת מַקִּיף שֶׁלְּמַעְלָה מֵהִשְׁתַּלְשְׁלוּת וְכֵלִים (וְלָכֵן אֵינָהּ נִקְלֶטֶת בִּסְפִירַת הַמַּלְכוּת בִּפְנִימִיּוּתָהּ לְפִי שֶׁהִיא לְמַעְלָה מֵהַגְבָּלַת הַכֵּלִים שֶׁלָּהּ).

אֲבָל מִכָּל מָקוֹם, הַמְשָׁכָה זוֹ הִיא בְּחִינַת חִיצוֹנִית, שֶׁהִיא רַק הֶאָרָה בִּלְבָד. מַה שֶּׁאֵין כֵּן עַל יְדֵי הַהַמְשָׁכָה

---

mission brings one to even greater heights. At this point, we return to the subject at hand, the transmission from *z'a* to *malchut*, explaining that this is due to the inherent advantage of *malchut* over *z'a* at its root. We will also learn that since this advantage is revealed only by *z'a*, the transmitter, it is imperative for an initial ("external") transmission from *z'a* to *malchut* to actually take place; only then can the virtue of the recipient come to light, thus drawing out the essence.

72. KEILIM. In the *seder hishtalshelut*, the order or chain of worlds, divine energy is given to the various levels of creation through a process of gradual and ordered descent and downward gradation, by means of numerous contractions. This energy is often called "light" in Kabbalah and Chas-

idus. Together with this metaphor of light, and inseparable from it, is that of *keilim*, literally, "vessels," or "instruments." These refer to the gradual levels in which the energy or light is manifest and expressed. For light *per se* is invisible; it becomes perceptible only in conjunction with something that reflects the light; i.e. a *keili*, "vessel." For example, the power of vision is the light, the eye is the vessel; the mind is the light, the brain is the vessel; the idea is the light, the words conveying it are the vessels.

However, there exists a quality of energy that is of too lofty a caliber to conform to *any* process of gradation or "vessel." This energy only encompasses the vessels it comes into contact with—as a *makif*—and is thus considered "external," as explained above, fns. 14 & 16.

does integrate internally within *malchut*, one reaches far higher (than the realm of *makif*).

MALCHUT AT ITS ROOT

To explain:[73] *Malchut* is rooted higher than *z'a*.[74] The root of
z'a is external *keter*, while the root of *malchut* is internal *keter*.
Although regarding *z'a* too, it states, "*z'a* is united with and
depends on *atik*"[75] [which is internal *keter*]—this does not refer to the essence of *atik* (but to its exterior).[76]

Conversely, *malchut* is rooted in the interior of *atik*,[77]
known as *radla*.[78]

Nevertheless, because *malchut* descends to a lower level
than *z'a*, its [lofty] root is hidden,[79] becoming exposed only

---

73. To understand the following section, an introduction is in order:

The first and highest *sefirah* is
called *keter* (lit, crown). *Keter* is the
"intermediary" between *Or Ein Sof*
and the worlds in the sense that it is
the lowest level of the Creator and the
highest level of creation. As such it
comprises two primary aspects—the
inner aspect of *keter*, which is called
atik or *atik yomin*, and the outer aspect, called *arich anpin*. The very
highest level of *atik* (*keter*, *chochmah*,
and *binah* of *atik*) is called *radla* (see
below fn. 78), where G-d's infinite
light rests, and is "G-d's delight."

Arich anpin is essentially the expression of "G-d's will and purpose"
in emanating that plane of reality. In
other words, the outer aspect of the
keter of *Atzilut* is the expression of
G-d's will and purpose in emanating
Atzilut, and the outer aspect of the
keter of *Beriah* is the expression of G-
d's will and purpose in the creation of
Beriah, and so on.

Arich anpin (external *keter*) is the
source for *chochmah* and *binah*,
which, in turn, transmit to *z'a* (*mid-*

dot). However, the *original* root of *z'a*
is in *atik*, surpassing *arich anpin*.

In human terms, emotions result
from intellect, yet after the emotions
are born, they may possess more en-
thusiasm than would have been ex-
pected by the intellectual stimulus.
The reason for this is that the root of
the emotions surpasses that of intellect (see also above, fn. 24). So intellect only stimulates the *expression* of
the emotions, but does not actually
create them.

Malchut, however, is rooted in *radla*. In human terms, the root of speech
surpasses that of emotions. As we see,
when one speaks words of love, this
arouses even greater love than before,
because speech is rooted in the essence
of the soul, conforming to the rule,
"the end is wedged in the beginning,
and the beginning is wedged in the
end" (*Sefer Yetzirah* 1:7). Hence, although *malchut* is actually lower than
z'a, it is specifically through *malchut*
that creation comes into being, there-
by fulfilling G-d's desire for a dwelling place in the lower realms.

So in contrast to *z'a* being a revela-

פְּנִימִית, שֶׁמִּתְקַבֶּלֶת בְּמַלְכוּת בִּפְנִימִיּוּתָהּ, מַגִּיעִים לְמַעְלָה יוֹתֵר (מִבְּחִינַת הַמַּקִּיף).

וְהָעִנְיָן הוּא, דְּשֹׁרֶשׁ הַמַּלְכוּת הוּא לְמַעְלָה מִשֹּׁרֶשׁ זָ"אⁱᶢ. דְּשֹׁרֶשׁ הַזָ"א הוּא מֵחִיצוֹנִיּוּת הַכֶּתֶר וְשֹׁרֶשׁ הַמַּלְכוּת הוּא מִפְּנִימִיּוּת הַכֶּתֶר. וַהֲגַם שֶׁגַּם בְּזָ"א אִיתְּמַרⁱᵈ זָ"א בְּעַתִּיקָא אֲחִיד וְתַלְיָא, הֲרֵי יָדוּעַ שֶׁאֵין הַכַּוָּונָה בָּזֶה עַל עַתִּיק מַמָּשׁ (רַק חִיצוֹנִיּוּת עַתִּיק).

מַה שֶּׁאֵין כֵּן שֹׁרֶשׁ הַמַּלְכוּת הִיא בִּפְנִימִיּוּת עַתִּיק, רַדְלָ"א [רֵישָׁא דְּלָא אִתְיְדַע]ⁱᶢ.

אֲבָל מִכָּל מָקוֹם, מִצַּד יְרִידָתָהּ לְמַטָּה הֲרֵי שָׁרְשָׁהּ הוּא

---

tion of G-dliness, *malchut* expresses G-d's Essence and inner will.

This explains the greatness of the transmission to *malchut* (the recipient), as elaborated in context of all the examples cited above in the main text. In all other instances of transmission, there are only revelations of "light," whereas in the transmission to *malchut*, G-d's Essence is actually transmitted.

74. **Regarding all this, see** *Sefer Hamaamarim 5659*, p. 11 [*Forces in Creation* (Kehot, 2003), pp. 32-4].

75. See *Zohar* III:292a.

76. Hence the expression, "united with and *depends* on *atik*," for *z'a* is not entirely one with *atik*, but rather with the quality of *atik* as it is transmitted into *arich anpin*, the outer aspect of *keter*. See reference in fn. 80, below.

77. I.e., the *interior* of internal *keter*.

78. **See source cited in fn. 74.**

RADLA. Acronym for *reisha d'lo ityada*, "the unknown beginning." This is a Kabbalistic term indicating the deepest and innermost level of the Essence of G-d which is entirely unknowable—not only because of its profundity, but because it is utterly beyond the realm of knowledge. Chasidus recognizes the bounds of intellect as innate. Intellect is a manifestation, a "power" of the soul or a *sefirah* of G-d, and is not Essence. Essence in turn transcends intellect. G-d's Essence is beyond knowledge because knowledge itself originates on a lower plane than G-d's Essence.

And with the transmission from *z'a* to *malchut*, G-d's *Essence* is actually transmitted. This is possible due to the greatness of the recipient—*malchut*, rooted in such a lofty realm.

79. Therefore, *malchut* on its own is unable to express and reveal its potential for G-d's Essence, but "depends" on *z'a* for that.

through *z'a*.[80] And it is specifically through this [exposure] that the *sefirah* of *malchut* can rise higher than *z'a*.[81]

ORDER OF TRANSMISSION

This is the meaning of "the order of the transmission": First there must be the transmission of *z'a* into *malchut* in a manner that expresses the transcendence of *z'a* over *malchut* (i.e., that it is only *z'a* that can reveal *malchut's* root).[82]

On the other hand, since the transmission takes place due to (the quality of) *z'a*, it does have some relationship to *hishtalshelut*[83] [similar to the aforementioned explanation (Ch. 3) regarding the "Thirteen Garments of the Beard"].

FROM MALCHUT TO Z'A

But when the transmission is internal and received by *malchut* in its interior, the root of *malchut* can be reached. For the transmission is then due to (the greatness of) *malchut*, whose root is more sublime than the root of *z'a*.[84] And ultimately, *malchut* will transmit into *z'a*, [in the spirit of] *An accomplished woman is the crown of her husband.*[85]

---

80. **See at length, the discourse entitled** *L'chol tichlah, 5659* [*Sefer Hamaamarim 5659*, p. 97 ff].

81. Thus, the union between *z'a* and *malchut* is *imperative*: The potential for revelation is provided by the giver, who reveals the great quality of the recipient. Subsequently, the root of the recipient, which transcends the level of the giver, becomes exposed.

82. There are two stages in the transmission from *z'a* to *malchut*, as mentioned above: the external transmission, wherein it remains in an encompassing (*makif*) form; and the internal transmission, wherein it is "tailored" for the recipient (*malchut*) and integrated within it.

Although in the first stage the transmission is beyond the capacity of the recipient and thus remains in *makif* form, this stage is necessary. For it is only possible to expose the recipient's greatness through "light" and "revelation"—qualities found only in the giver (even if of such lofty caliber that they cannot be contained within the recipient).

83. At the same time, the light is "beyond the *capacity of the recipient*," i.e., it *does* have *some* relationship to the recipient, albeit in a *makif*-type of form (as discussed above, fn. 49). It is therefore not a means to reach G-d's Essence.

בְּהֶעְלֵם, וְגִילּוּי שֹׁרֶשׁ הַמַּלְכוּת הוּא עַל יְדֵי ז"א דַוְקָא⁸⁴, וְעַל
יְדֵי זֶה גּוּפָא סְפִירַת הַמַּלְכוּת מִתְעַלֵּית לְמַעְלָה מִז"א.

וְזֶהוּ עִנְיַן סֵדֶר הַהַמְשָׁכָה, דְּתְחִילָה צְרִיכָה לִהְיוֹת
הַמְשָׁכַת הַז"א בְּמַלְכוּת בְּאוֹפֶן שֶׁיּוּרְגַּשׁ עִנְיַן הַז"א שֶׁלְּמַעְלָה
מִמַּלְכוּת (שֶׁדַּוְקָא עַל יָדוֹ הוּא גִילּוּי שֹׁרֶשׁ הַמַּלְכוּת).

אֲבָל מִכָּל מָקוֹם, מִכֵּיוָן שֶׁהַהַמְשָׁכָה הִיא מִצַּד (מַעֲלַת)
ז"א, יֵשׁ לָהּ שַׁיָּיכוּת לְהִשְׁתַּלְשְׁלוּת [עַל דֶּרֶךְ הַנַּ"ל (סְעִיף ג)
בְּעִנְיַן י"ג תִּקּוּנֵי דִּיקְנָא].

וְדַוְקָא עַל יְדֵי הַהַמְשָׁכָה פְּנִימִית שֶׁמִּתְקַבֶּלֶת בְּמַלְכוּת
בִּפְנִימִיּוּתָהּ, הֲרֵי מִכֵּיוָן שֶׁהַהַמְשָׁכָה זוֹ הִיא מִצַּד (מַעֲלַת)
הַמַּלְכוּת, הֲרֵי מַגִּיעִים עַל יְדֵי זֶה לְשֹׁרֶשׁ הַמַּלְכוּת שֶׁלְּמַעְלָה
מִשֹּׁרֶשׁ ז"א, וְעַד שֶׁהַמַּלְכוּת מַשְׁפִּיעַ בְּז"א, אֵשֶׁת חַיִל עֲטֶרֶת
בַּעְלָהּ⁸⁵.

---

84. In order to awaken *malchut*, and particularly its source, and to enable a transmission of G-d's Essence, the transmission needs to be an internal one. In a transmission of this type, the light constricts itself and becomes "tailored" to the limitations of the recipient, taking into consideration the quality and character of the recipient. Thus, since this form of transmission fulfills the will of G-d's Essence, i.e., of having a dwelling place in the lower realms, it is specifically in this manner that G-d's Essence (which is *radla*, the root of *malchut*) can be attained and subsequently transmitted.

85. **Proverbs 12:4.** At this point *mal-*chut becomes a crown—a *keter* and a *makif*—for *z'a*, its "husband," for additional light from the root of *malchut* is then transmitted to *z'a*.

* * *

Thus, the discourse has presented its main point: The transmission from *z'a* to *malchut* is "external," in a *makif*-type form, transcending *hishtalshelut*. This paves the way for a transmission into the interior of *malchut*. This internal transmission will ultimately cause *malchut* to reach its own root (*keter*), and subsequently, *malchut* (the recipient), will give to *z'a* (the giver), and raise it "ever higher" to a realm otherwise unattainable on its own.

6.

THE TWO FACES OF SHABBAT

This, then, is the explanation of the two extremes regarding Shabbat, cited [by my father-in-law, the Rebbe] (at the beginning of his discourse).

[On one hand] Shabbat is called "queen,"[4] and refers to *malchut*,[8] which is lower than the other *sefirot*, and receives from them—as the saying,[86] "the moon that has no light of its own."[7]

[Similarly, our Sages said (regarding Shabbat) that specifically "one who toils on Erev Shabbat will [have what to] eat on Shabbat."[87]]

But on the other hand, "all the days [of the ensuing week] are blessed from Shabbat."[88] I.e., besides the fact that Shabbat is holier than the rest of the week, Shabbat actually *transmits* to them.[89]

SHABBAT AS RECIPIENT

The explanation is: The seven days of the week are the Seven Days of Creation.[90] The six weekdays are [rooted] in *z'a*, as it is written, *Six days G-d made [the heavens and the earth]*,[91] and, as the *Zohar* states, "Each day itself did the work of that day,"[92] and Shabbat is *malchut* (as mentioned).

Therefore, because *malchut* descended *lower*,[93] and particularly due to her descent into *B'YA*[94]—"her feet go down

---

86. *Zohar* I:249b, et al.

87. *Avodah Zara* 3a. See below, fn. 98.

88. See *Zohar* II:63b; 88a.

89. So how do we reconcile these two statements? Does Shabbat (*malchut*) "receive" from the six weekdays (*z'a*), or does Shabbat "give" to them?

90. Or, in other words, the seven *sefirot* of *chesed, gevurah, tiferet, netzach,*

hod, yesod, and *malchut*. On each day of the Seven Days of Creation a different attribute was in use to create the creations of that particular day.

91. **Exodus 20:11.**

92. *Zohar* III:94b, et al. The source of creation is G-d's *middot*. Just as human emotions express one's feelings, G-d's *middot* serve as His modes of expression with regard to creation.

The *Zohar* explains that this is alluded to in the verse, *For six days G-d*

ו.

וְיֵשׁ לוֹמַר שֶׁזֶּהוּ גַּם כֵּן הַבֵּיאוּר בָּזֶה שֶׁמֵּבִיא (בִּתְחִלַּת הַמַּאֲמָר) ב' קְצָווֹת בְּעִנְיָן הַשַּׁבָּת,

דְּהַשַּׁבָּת נִקְרֵאת מַלְכָּה שֶׁהִיא סְפִירַת הַמַּלְכוּת שֶׁלְּמַטָּה מִכָּל הַסְּפִירוֹת וּמְקַבֶּלֶת מֵהֶן, כַּמַּאֲמָר[ל״ז] סִיהֲרָא לֵית לָהּ מִגַּרְמָהּ כְּלוּם

[וּכְמַאֲמָר רַז״ל[ל״ח] (גַּבֵּי שַׁבָּת) דְּדַוְקָא מִי שֶׁטָּרַח בְּעֶרֶב שַׁבָּת יֹאכַל בְּשַׁבָּת],

וּלְאִידָךְ הֲרֵי כּוּלְהוּ יוֹמִין מִתְבָּרְכִין מֵהַשַּׁבָּת[ל״ט], הַיְנוּ דְּלֹא זוֹ בִּלְבָד שֶׁשַּׁבָּת מְקוּדָּשׁ מִכָּל הַיָּמִים, אֶלָּא עוֹד זֹאת, שֶׁהִיא מַשְׁפִּיעָה בָּהֶם.

אַךְ הָעִנְיָן הוּא, דְּז' יְמֵי הַשָּׁבוּעַ הֵם שִׁבְעַת יְמֵי הַבִּנְיָן, דְּשֵׁשֶׁת יְמֵי הַחוֹל הֵם בְּזָ״א כְּמוֹ שֶׁכָּתוּב[מ] שֵׁשֶׁת יָמִים עָשָׂה הוי' אֶת הַשָּׁמַיִם וְאֶת הָאָרֶץ וְאִיתָא בְּזֹהַר[מ״א] כָּל יוֹמָא וְיוֹמָא עָבִיד עֲבִידְתֵּיהּ, וְשַׁבָּת הִיא מַלְכוּת (כַּנ״ל).

וְלָכֵן, מִצַּד זֶה שֶׁהַמַּלְכוּת יָרְדָה לְמַטָּה, וּבִפְרָט מִצַּד יְרִידָתָהּ לְבִי״ע [לִבְרִיאָה יְצִירָה עֲשִׂיָּה] דְּרַגְלֶיהָ יוֹרְדוֹת

---

made the heaven and the earth. If the intent was to relate that G-d created the world in six days, then grammatically the Hebrew should have read, *"b'sheshet yamim"* (*"in* six days"). However, the wording is *sheshet yamim*, implying that G-d made six "days"—these being His *middot*—which facilitated the creation.

93. I.e., lower than *z'a*, the other *sefirot*.

94. *B'YA* is an acronym for *Beriah*,

Yetzirah, *Asiyah*, the three lower worlds, following *Atzilut*.

THE FOUR WORLDS. Kabbalah and Chasidus explain the phenomenon of the creation of a finite physical universe by an Infinite Creator with the concept of *tzimtzum*—contraction and concealment. G-d effected a series of concealments of His presence and infinitude, resulting ultimately, in the creation of our physical universe, through a virtually total concealment of G-d. The non-corporeal intermediate steps between the Crea-

[unto death]"[95]—Shabbat (i.e., *malchut*) receives from the six weekdays (*z'a*).[96] This corresponds to the task of refining (the animal soul and all physical matter) during the six weekdays.[97]

SHABBAT AS GIVER

However, after (and by means of) this task, *malchut* rises from *B'YA* until its root and source (on Shabbat).[98] It then rises

---

tor and this material world are called "Worlds," referring to the basic levels of spiritual existence in the creative process. The differentiation reflects their level of concealment of the divine light, the higher worlds receiving in a more revealed form (see also above, fns. 44 & 69).

In general, there are Four Worlds: *Atzilut* (World of Emanation, a state of proximity and relative unity with G-d); *Beriah* (World of Creation); *Yetzirah* (World of Formation); *Asiyah* (World of Action or Making, the final stage in the creative process). The four worlds have been compared to the elements inherent to building a house. Four stages are necessary: 1) A general idea, as yet undefined; 2) A definite idea of the house in one's mind; 3) The architectural plan or design; 4) The actual building of the house (*Tanya*, Bi-lingual Edition, p. 343 fn. 3; p. 844 (Kehot, 1998)).

"Higher" (or "Supernal") and "Lower" refer to stages closer or more distant from the Creator, with a greater or lesser awareness of Him (not, of course, implying physical distance). Lower Worlds appear to be independent entities apart from the Creator.

Through the performance of *mitzvot* and subordination of the physical world to the divine purpose, all Worlds are elevated, and experience a clearer apprehension of G-d. See J.

Immanuel Schochet, *Mystical Concepts in Chassidism*, Ch. 2 (*Tzimtzum*) and Ch. 4 (Worlds).

95. *Malchut* of *Atzilut* as it stands in *Atzilut* is far removed from comparison or relationship with *B'YA*. Therefore, when *malchut* of *Atzilut* descends to *B'YA* in order to vivify them, it is called "*her feet*—i.e., *malchut*, the lowest level ('feet')—*go down to death*—i.e., *B'YA*, as opposed to *Atzilut* ('life')."

B'YA, in comparison to *Atzilut*, are called "death," as it is written, *See, I have placed before you this day the life and the good, the death and the evil* (Deuteronomy 30:15). The four terms in this verse are descriptions of the spiritual and physical. The spiritual is life and good; the physical is death and evil. Hence, *her feet go down to death*, for *Beriah* is considered physical in relation to the "spiritual" *Atzilut*—not in the least comparable to it (*Overcoming Folly*, pp. 306-8 (Kehot, 2006)).

Now, by *malchut* of *Atzilut* descending to vivify *B'YA*, it also refines *B'YA*. For when the latter worlds sense the G-dliness in *malchut*, they become subjugated to that G-dliness, and any G-dly sparks within them are refined and elevated. This is what takes place during the six weekdays. However, on Shabbat *malchut* returns to its root in *Atzilut*, taking all the re-

כו׳, הַשַּׁבָּת (מַלְכוּת) מְקַבֶּלֶת מִשֵּׁשֶׁת יְמֵי הַחוֹל (ז"א), שֶׁהוּא
עִנְיַן עֲבוֹדַת הַבֵּירוּרִים (בֵּירוּר הַנֶּפֶשׁ הַבַּהֲמִית וְכָל הַדְּבָרִים
הַגַּשְׁמִיִּים) דְּשֵׁשֶׁת יְמֵי הַחוֹל.

אָמְנָם לְאַחֲרֵי (וְעַל יְדֵי) עֲבוֹדָה זוֹ נַעֲשָׂה (בְּשַׁבָּת)
עֲלִיַּית הַמַּלְכוּת מבי"ע עַד עֵלֶיהָ לְשָׁרְשָׁהּ וּמְקוֹרָהּ, וְאָז

---

fined sparks along with it, as now that they have been refined, they can rise to a loftier level. Hence, Shabbat (*malchut*) receives from the six weekdays (*z'a*).

96. Each of G-d's *middot* correspond to a day of the week, and *malchut* corresponds to Shabbat. Being the lowest *middah*, or *sefirah*, it naturally *receives* from all the other *sefirot*. In this sense, Shabbat would serve as a recipient from the previous six days of the week.

97. AVODAT HABIRURIM. The divine attributes—*sefirot*—in their original pristine state, as they emanate from the *Ein Sof*, are absolute, distinct, and mutually exclusive. This absolute stance prevents them from tolerating one another. Hence, *chesed* has no relation to *gevurah*; they are opposite and incompatible, like fire and water. In this state, the *sefirot* are at the height of their intensity; each one a separate potency, unqualified and unmitigated.

However, the *sefirot* were conceived as two aspects, namely *or* (light) and *k'li* (vessel), standing in relation to each other as form to matter. But in the pristine state, the light was too intense to be controlled or contained. This led to *shevirat hakeilim*, the "breaking of the vessels," a process whereby the intense divine light

was substantially shut off, as it were, and "sparks" thereof fell from the upper realm into our physical world.

The "breaking of the vessels" gave rise to a new, orderly world, where the *sefirot* are integrated and intertwined. The "light" and the "vessel" became compatible in this stage—as explained above, fn. 72.

And the sparks? Having fallen into mundane objects in this physical world, it became man's duty to "elevate" these sparks back to the realm of holiness. Until these sparks of G-dliness are elevated, they remain "trapped," as it were, in exile. Hence the purpose of our lengthy exile—to "redeem" those sparks which require "elevation" and "refinement." This process is termed *avodat habirurim*, "the service of refinement," which is performed by utilizing all permitted worldly things with which one comes in contact—during the six weekdays—for a holy, G-dly purpose.

98. During the week a person's task is to work with the material world, and refine the divine sparks trapped within it. On Shabbat, however, one "reaps the benefits" of this work, by enjoying the delight and pleasure generated from the week's work, when the divine sparks rise to a higher spiritual level.

Hence, our Sages say, "One who toils on Erev Shabbat will [have what higher than *z'a* to the extent that it actually transmits to the six weekdays (*z'a*), for "all the days [of the ensuing week] are blessed from Shabbat."[99]

7.

This, then, is the meaning of *Come, my Beloved, to meet the bride; let us welcome the Shabbat*[100]—it is a request by the souls of the Jewish people that there be a transmission of *z'a* into *malchut.*[101]

"WELCOMING THE SHABBAT"

This transmission begins by *Come, my Beloved, to meet the bride*—a mere "coming"[102], but will later cause *let us welcome the Shabbat*—an internal transmission, *"pnei Shabbat,"*[103] revealing the innermost core of *malchut* to the extent that its root in *atik* is revealed too. Hence, *let us welcome*, in the plural, meaning that *z'a* also receives from (the root of) *malchut*[104]—[in the spirit of] *An accomplished woman is the crown of her husband.*[105]

---

to] eat on Shabbat," which in Kabbalistic terms refers to the spiritual "food" or gain which is enjoyed on Shabbat by one who refined physicality during the previous week.

99. So the fact that *malchut* possesses the ability to be a "giver"—enabling the sparks to rise to a higher level—is only due to having previously been a "recipient" from *z'a*, during the previous week. But then, *malchut*, remaining with its longing to return to its source even upon descent, can actually cause the sparks to rise to their source, the Essence of G-d.

Thus, Shabbat becomes a "giver" to the subsequent week, blessing it by causing it to be greater than the previous week.

In term of divine service, through transforming all one's physical mat-

ters into conduits for G-dliness, one rises "ever higher," as discussed above, end of Chapter 4.

* * *

To draw some comparisons between the aforementioned examples and the subject of this chapter:

Transmission from the giver to the receiver: teacher to student, father to son, prayer to the physical matters of the day, weekday to Shabbat, *z'a* to *malchut.*

Ultimately, this transmission reveals "essence" and causes the receiver to become the giver: student enhances teacher, son awakens father's inner love, transformation of all physical matter to holiness, Shabbat elevates ensuing week, *malchut* becomes crown for *z'a.*

The following chapter explains this concept in relation to a groom and

מִתְעַלֵּית לְמַעְלָה מִזָּ"א עַד שֶׁמַּשְׁפַּעַת גַּם לְכָל שֵׁשֶׁת יְמֵי הַחוֹל (זָ"א), דְּמִינֵּיהּ מִתְבָּרְכִין כּוּלְּהוּ יוֹמִין.

ז.

וְזֶהוּ לְכָה דוֹדִי לִקְרַאת כַּלָּה פְּנֵי שַׁבָּת נְקַבְּלָה, שֶׁהוּא בַּקָּשַׁת נִשְׁמוֹת יִשְׂרָאֵל שֶׁתִּהְיֶה הַמְשָׁכַת הַזָּ"א בְּמַלְכוּת.

דִּתְחִילַּת הַהַמְשָׁכָה הִיא לְכָה דוֹדִי לִקְרַאת כַּלָּה, הֲלִיכָה בִּלְבָד, וְעַל יְדֵי זֶה פְּנֵי שַׁבָּת נְקַבְּלָה, שֶׁהוּא הַהַמְשָׁכָה פְּנִימִית, פְּנֵי שַׁבָּת[מ״ג], שֶׁמִּתְגַּלֶּה בְּחִינַת פְּנִימִיּוּת הַמַּלְכוּת וְעַד כְּמוֹ שֶׁהִיא מוּשְׁרֶשֶׁת בְּעַתִּיק. וְלָכֵן נְקַבְּלָה לְשׁוֹן רַבִּים, שֶׁגַּם זָ"א מְקַבֵּל מִ(וֹשֶׁרֶשׁ הַ)מַּלְכוּת[מ״ג], אֵשֶׁת חַיִל עֲטֶרֶת בַּעֲלָה.

---

bride. The groom transmits to the bride, but it is the bride who gives birth to offspring.

100. The discourse now returns to the discussion begun in Chapter 1, and describes how the concepts of "internal" and "external" connections relate to z'a and malchut—the spiritual counterparts of the groom and bride.

101. The bride, i.e., the souls of the Jewish people, request of the Groom (my Beloved), to transmit from Himself (z'a) to her (malchut).

102. The beginning of the transmission is that the groom merely moves toward the bride. However, this paves the way for the subsequent inner transmission.

103. In the Hebrew phrase of Lecha Dodi, the words for "let us welcome the Shabbat" are pnei Shabbat nekablah. The word pnei literally means "face," but can be etymologically related to the word penimiyut, meaning "the innermost core of." The discourse explains that the word pnei implies that the transmission is internal by nature—that a) there is an internal transmission from z'a to malchut, and b) the innermost core of malchut is revealed to the extent that its root, atik, is revealed as well.

See the aforementioned discourse, **Semuchim La'ad, 5680, (p. 6)** [Sefer Hamaamarim 5680, pp. 151-2].

104. **See there, beginning of Chapter 2.**

105. "Let us welcome," in the plural, implies that "both of us"—malchut and z'a—serve as recipients: Malchut receives from z'a, and then subsequently, z'a receives from malchut, as explained in the previous chapter.

GIVER AND RECEIVER

Just as it is on high, regarding *z'a* and *malchut*, so it applies
with every giver and receiver: The giver actually gains through
the receiver, [as in the aforementioned statement] "From my
students I learned more than from all the others."[106]

GROOM AND BRIDE

It particularly applies in regard to a physical groom and bride,
that through the internal transmission specifically, [will be
fulfilled the verse] *An accomplished woman is the crown of her
husband,*[107] and *Everything came from the earth.*[108]

This [union and internal transmission] elicits G-d's infinite power—with offspring that are upright and blessed,
children and grandchildren who are occupied with the Torah
and *mitzvot.*

106. See above, end of Chapter 2. See
also end of Chapters 3-6.

107. See above, end of Chapter
3—that this same concept applies to
every groom and bride: The groom
receives from the bride, for she is
called *the crown of her husband,* and
due to her quality of *malchut,* they
can together give birth to offspring.
Hence, the groom is elevated through
transmitting to the bride.

Thus the discourse here states, "It
particularly applies in regard to a
physical groom and bride": The way
to create *ex nihilo*—to "elicit G-d's
infinite power," i.e., "offspring that
are upright and blessed"—is specif-

וּכְמוֹ שֶׁהוּא לְמַעְלָה בֵּזַ"א וּמַלְכוּת, עַל דֶּרֶךְ זֶה הוּא בְּכָל
מַשְׁפִּיעַ וּמְקַבֵּל, שֶׁעַל יְדֵי הַמְקַבֵּל נִתוֹסֵף בְּהַמַּשְׁפִּיעַ,
וּמִתַּלְמִידֵי יוֹתֵר מִכּוּלָם.

וּבִפְרָט בְּחָתָן וְכַלָּה לְמַטָּה, שֶׁדַּוְקָא עַל יְדֵי הַהַמְשָׁכָה
פְּנִימִית, הִנֵּה אֵשֶׁת חַיִל עֲטֶרֶת בַּעְלָהּ, וְהַכֹּל הָיָה מִן הֶעָפָרᵐᶜ.

שֶׁעַל יְדֵי זֶה נִמְשָׁךְ כֹּחַ הָאֵין סוֹף בְּדוֹר יְשָׁרִים יְבוֹרָךְ
בְּבָנִים וּבְנֵי בָנִים עוֹסְקִים בַּתּוֹרָה וּמִצְווֹת.

---

ically by the groom uniting with the *bride*.

The role of the groom is to reveal the bride's ability to procreate, whereas the role of the bride is to actually produce the "essence"—the offspring.

108. Ecclesiastes 3:20. See *Likkutei Torah, Shir Hashirim* 40a; *Iggeret*

Hakodesh, 20, end.

True, earth is essentially a recipient, for everyone steps on it. However, although earth is inert as well as the *lowliest* level of creation, because it is rooted in the lowest *sefirah, malchut*, it possesses G-d's procreative power—"creation *ex nihilo*" (see fn. 73).

HEBREW NOTES

הערות לד"ה לכה דודי תרפ"ט

א. המאמר מיוסד על ד"ה לכה דודי במאמרי אדה"ז על מאמרי רז"ל ע' תנה ואילך. ועם הוספות וביאורים – ד"ה סמוכים לעד פר"ת (סה"מ פר"ת ע' קמט ואילך).

לכמה ענינים המבוארים בהמאמר – ראה ד"ה לכה דודי תשי"ד (סה"מ מלוקט ח"א ע' מג ואילך.) ש"כנראה הוא מיוסד (ביאור) על ד"ה לכה דודי תרפ"ט" (מהקדמת המו"ל להמאמר – סה"מ מלוקט שם ע' מב).

ב. ב"סדר קבלת שבת".

ג. ראה לקמן בפנים המאמר.

ד. בראשית א, כו. ראה של"ה בהקדמה (ט, ב. י, א). לקו"ת ויקרא ד, ב. ובכ"מ.

ה. ראה סה"מ תר"ן ע' שנח. תרנ"ז ריש ע' קעז. המשך תרס"ו ע' קנז. סה"מ עטר"ת ע' שעא. סה"מ תרפ"ה ע' סא. תרפ"ט ע' 38. ע' 168. תרצ"ט ע' 62. תרצ"ז ריש ע' 235. ועוד.

ו. כ"ה בכ"מ בדא"ח בשם הזהר. – לע"ע לא מצאתיו בל' זה. וראה זח"ג קד, ב. זח"א צ, סע"ב. רכז, ב. רלג, ב. זח"ב צו, ב. זח"ג סא, ב (הערת כ"ק אדמו"ר בסה"מ תרצ"ו שם).

ז. ח"ג ה, א. וראה זהר חי"א רנו, א. ח"ג סט, א. איכ"ר פ"ה, יט.

ח. בראשית א, כז-כח.

ט. זהר ח"ב סג, ב. פח, א.

י. בהבא לקמן – ראה גם מאמרי אדמו"ר דרושי חתונה ח"א ע"ר קסו.

יא. בזהר שלפנינו: ומשתיו.

יב. ישעי' ד, ה. וראה ד"ה כי על כל כבוד חופה בלקו"ת שה"ש מז, ב ואילך. סידור עם דא"ח קכח, ד ואילך. מאמרי אדמו"ר האמצעי דרושי חתונה ח"א ע' א ואילך. שם ע' ז.

יג. שה"ש ג, יא. תענית כו, ב.

יד. מלאכי א, ב.

טו. תהלים פד, ג.

טז. בהבא לקמן (עד סוף פ"ב) – ראה מאמרי אדה"ז וסה"מ פר"ת שבהערה 1.

יז. כן הוא [רבה] בש"ס ועין יעקב. אבל בתניא פ"י [יא, ב] הביא גירסת רבינו חננאל, וכן הוא בילקוט שמעוני [מלכים ב] רמז רכז רבא. ויש לעיין בד"ס ובשבת ל, ב (הערת כ"ק אדמו"ר בסה"מ פר"ת הנ"ל הערה 1). – בתורת חיים שבהערה הבאה ומאמרי אדמו"ר האמצעי קונטרסים ע' שפא: רבא.

יח. תורת חיים תולדות ב, ד. צויין בסה"מ פר"ת שם.

יט. סוכה כא, ב. ע"ז יט, ב.

כ. מלכים ב ג, יא.

כא. ברכות כב, א. וראה תו"א יתרו סז, ב.

כב. יתרו כ, טו.

כג. פסחים קיז, א. שבת ל, ב. יל"ש מלכים ב רמז רכז.

כד. "מקור משל זה הוא באור תורה להרב המגיד (פה, סע"ד [עה"פ (הושע יא, ג) אנכי תרגלתי לאפרים קחם על זרועותיו]" – ד"ה לכה דודי תשי"ד הנ"ל הערה 1 פ"ג (סה"מ מלוקט שם ע' מד.). וראה גם (בנוסף להמצויין בהערה 1) לקו"ת פינחס שבהערה הבאה.

כה. בהבא לקמן — ראה לקו"ת פינחס פ, ב.

כו. פסוק ג.

כז. בכל הבא לקמן — השווה לקו"ת שם עט, ד ואילך.

כח. תנחומא פקודי ג. תקו"ז תס"ט (ק, ב. קא, א).

כט. בראשית א, ה.

ל. ראה סה"מ תרפ"ח ע' קנג ובהערה 2.

לא. מיכה ז, ח (כ"ה גם בלקו"ת פינחס שם. אבל בפסוק ליתא תיבת גם).

לב. פסחים נד, ב.

לג. שם קיג, ב.

לד. ישעי' ס, ב.

לה. פרדס שער יב (שער הנתיבות) פ"ב. ראשית חכמה שער התשובה פ"ו ד"ה
והמרגיל (קכא, ב). של"ה פט, א (דאיתא בזהר): קפט, א (ומרומז בזהר): שח, ב. שו"ת
חכם צבי סי"ח. שער היחוד והאמונה רפ"ו. לקו"ת פ' ראה כב, סע"ב ואילך.

לו. ראה זהר ח"ג רנז, סע"ב. פרדס שער א (שער עשר ולא תשע) פ"ט. שער היחוד
והאמונה פרק ד, ז.

לז. ראה גם סה"מ עטר"ת ע' שס. ד"ה שימני כחותם תר"ץ פרק ב (סה"מ
קונטרסים ח"א צו, ב). סה"מ תרצ"ז ע' 149. ובכ"מ.

לח. איכה ג, כג. ראה ילקוט שמעוני תהלים רמז תשב. שו"ע אדה"ז או"ח מהדו"ק
ס"ד ס"א.

לט. ראה בהנסמן בהערות 41-43.

מ. תו"א תרומה עט, סע"ד. סה"מ תרפ"ג ע' רטו. ובכ"מ.

מא. ישעי' ב, כב. ברכות יד, א.

מב. בכ"ז — ראה (נוסף להמצויין לעיל הערה 27) מאמרי אדה"ז על פרשיות
התורה ע' תשמז: על מאמרי רז"ל ע' יז. דרך חיים שער התפלה פרק פג. אוה"ת
בראשית ח"ז תתרכ, א. הקדמה ללקו"ת לג' פרשיות לאדמו"ר מהר"ש.

מג. ראה רמ"ז לזהר ח"ב קפב, א (צויין בלקו"ת הנ"ל הערה 27). זהר חדש רות צ,
ד. מקומות שנסמנו בהערה הקודמת.

מד. ברכות רפ"ה.

מה. כ"ה בכ"מ בדא"ח בשם רש"י "הכנעה ושפלות" (סה"מ תרס"ה ס"ע קצד.
המשך תרס"ו ע' תפז. סה"מ תרע"ח ריש ע' צד. שם ע' תלג. תש"ז ע' 203. ועוד).

אבל בפרש"י לפנינו אין תיבת "ושפלות" (וכן אינה בהעתקת לשון רש"י באגה"ת
פ"י (צט, ב). מאמרי אדה"ז על מארז"ל (ע' מב. מד). אוה"ת על מארז"ל (ע' יג. יח).
ועוד).

ונ"ל שהכוונה במקומות הנ"ל רק לתוספת ביאור על פרש"י בענין ההכנעה.

וראה ספר המכתם לברכות שם: "הכנעה ושפלות הרוח". וראה רמ"א ושו"ע אדה"ז
או"ח סצ"ח ס"א. לקו"ת בלק עא, ג. שערי תשובה לאדמו"ר האמצעי שער התפלה פ"ב
(כג, סע"ב ואילך). ובכ"מ. — עפ"י הערת כ"ק אדמו"ר בסה"מ תרע"ח שם (ס"ע צג
ואילך), תש"ז שם. לקו"ש חלק לד ע' 69 הערה 18.

מו. ראה מאמרי אדה"ז וסה"מ פר"ת שבהערה 1.

מז. תענית ז, א.

מח. משלי יב, ד.

מט. שם יח, כב (ושם: ויפק רצון מה'). וראה אוה"ת נ"ך עה"פ (ח"א ע' תרטו
ואילך).

הערות לד״ה לכה דודי תשי״ד

א. נדפס בסה״מ קונטרסים ח״א כ, א ואילך. וז״ע [בשנת תשל״ט] עוה״פ בקונטרס בפ״ע [סה״מ תרפ״ט ע׳ 81 ואילך].

ב. פט״ז.

ג. שם ס״ב.

ד. לשון הכתוב — ישעי׳ ד, ה.

ה. ראה בכ״ז בסידור ובלקו״ת שה״ש ד״ה כי על כל כבוד.

ו. ד״ה שמח תשמח תרנ״ז ע׳ 90 ואילך [סה״מ תרנ״ז ע׳ רסז]. ובכ״מ. וראה גם לקו״ת שם מ, רע״א.

ז. פסחים קיז, א. וש״נ.

ח. סוכה כא, ב. ע״ז יט, ב.

ט. ד״ה ואלה תולדות ס״ו (ב, ד).

י. ס״א [נדפס בקונטרס בפ״ע — קה״ת תשי״ב [ובסה״מ פר״ת ע׳ קמח].

יא. וידוע ג״כ הסיפור, שבאחד המאמרים שאמר כ״ק אדמו״ר (מהורש״ב) נ״ע ביחידות לבנו כ״ק מו״ח אדמו״ר אמר ענין (משל מכח הציור שבנפש) בדרך אפשר, ואח״כ כ״ק מו״ח אדמו״ר אצל חותנו הרה״ח וכו׳ ר׳ אברהם בקעשענוב, ובקשו לחזור דא״ח, באמרו: עפן נאר אויף דעם קראן וועט שוין גיסן, וחזר את מאמר הנ״ל וגם ענין הנ״ל בפשטות. כשחזר לליובאוויטש סיפר לאביו את כל המאורע, ושאלהו כ״ק אדמו״ר (מהורש״ב) נ״ע, הא מנין לך? הרי אמרתי רק בדרך אפשר? וענה לו: מה שאצלך בדרך אפשר נעשה אצלי דבר ודאי.

יב. סי״ב (ה, ג).

יג. המשך תרס״ו ע׳ צט ואילך. ד״ה והי׳ כי תבוא תרע״ה (בהמשך תער״ב ח״ב [ע׳ א׳קכג ואילך]).

יד. תענית ז, א. וראה לקמן סעיף ז׳.

טו. פה, סע״ד [עה״פ (הושע יא, ג) אנכי תרגלתי לאפרים קחם על זרועותיו].

טז. ועד״ז בלקו״ת פינחס פ, ב. ד״ה סמוכים לעד שם.

יז. בכללות השעשועים הו״ע הקירוב פנימי (כנ״ל. מד״ה לכה דודי תרפ״ט). אבל בערך הלימוד והשפעות פנימיות דהבן מאביו וכיו״ב, גם זה קירוב חיצוני.

יח. תהלים כה, ו. וראה ד״ה אשר ברא תרפ״ט פ״ג (בדרושי חתונה שם — כג, א [סה״מ תרפ״ט ע׳ 89].

יט. אוה״ת וירא צג, ב. המשך תרס״ו ע׳ רפה.

כ. ראה במפתחות לס׳ הצ״צ.

כא. ס״ג.

כב. ישעי׳ ב, כב.

כג. ברכות יד, א.

כד. לקו״ת פנחס עט, ד. הקדמה ללקו״ת לג״פ לאדמו״ר מהר״ש [נדפס באוה״ת בראשית (כרך ו) תתרכ, א ואילך].

כה. תו״א תרומה עט, סע״ד. ובכ״מ.

כו. כתר שם טוב (הוצאת קה״ת) סרי״ב.

כז. ברכות שם. טושו״ע (ואדה״ז) או״ח ספ״ט ס״ב (ס״ג).

כח. שעהמ״צ פ׳ יתרו. ל״ת פ׳ וירא. וראה זח״ג פג, א.

כט. כתובות קג, א.

ל. יתרו כ, יב.

לא. ראה לקו"ת האזינו עה, ב. ובכ"מ.

לב. משלי יד, ד.

לג. ראה בכ"ז — סה"מ תרנ"ט ע' יא.

לד. ראה זח"ג רצב, א.

לה. ראה באורוכה ד"ה לכל תכלה תרנ"ט [סה"מ תרנ"ט ע' צז ואילך].

לו. משלי יב, ד.

לז. זח"א רמט, ב. ובכ"מ.

לח. ע"ז ג, א.

לט. ראה זח"ב סג, ב. פח, א.

מ. יתרו שם, יא.

מא. ח"ג צד, ריש ע"ב. ועוד.

מב. ראה ד"ה סמוכים לעד הנ"ל (ע' 6 [ע' קנא-ב]).

מג. ראה שם רפ"ב.

מד. קהלת ג, כ. וראה לקו"ת שה"ש מ, א. אגה"ק סוס"כ.

ORDER OF THE BETROTHAL AND MARRIAGE BLESSINGS

ഛഗ൏ൟ൏ൟൣ

ORDER OF THE BETROTHAL AND
MARRIAGE BLESSINGS

The officiating Rabbi holds a cup of wine and recites the following blessings:

ברוך Blessed are You, Lord our God, King of the universe, who creates the fruit of the vine.

ברוך Blessed are You, Lord our God, King of the universe, who has sanctified us with His commandments and commanded us concerning illicit marriages, forbidden to us the betrothed and permitted to us those who are married to us by the rite of chupah and kiddushin (consecration). Blessed are You Lord, who sanctifies His people Israel through chupah and kiddushin.

The groom drinks of the wine, then the bride. The groom then betroths the bride with a ring and says:

הרי With this ring, you are consecrated to me according to the law of Moses and Israel.

The *ketubah* (marriage contract) is read, and the groom hands it to the bride. The cup is refilled, and the following blessings are recited:[1]

ברוך Blessed are You, Lord our God, King of the universe, who creates the fruit of the vine.

ברוך Blessed are You, Lord our God, King of the universe, who has created all things for His glory.

ברוך Blessed are You, Lord our God, King of the universe, Creator of man.

ברוך Blessed are You, Lord our God, King of the universe, who created man in His image, in the image [of His] likeness [He fashioned] his form, and prepared for him from his own self an everlasting edifice. Blessed are You Lord, Creator of man.

שוש May the barren one [Jerusalem] rejoice and be happy at the ingathering of her children to her midst in joy. Blessed are You Lord, who gladdens Zion with her children.

שמח Grant abundant joy to these loving friends, as You bestowed gladness upon Your created being in the Garden of Eden of old. Blessed are You Lord, who gladdens the groom and bride.

ברוך Blessed are You, Lord our God, King of the universe, who created joy and happiness, groom and bride, gladness, jubilation, cheer and delight, love, friendship, harmony and fellowship. Lord our God, let there speedily be heard in the cities of Judah and in the streets of Jerusalem the sound of joy and the sound of happiness, the sound of a groom and the sound of a bride, the sound of exultation of grooms from under their chupah, and youths from their joyous banquets. Blessed are You Lord, who gladdens the groom with the bride.

The groom, then the bride drink from the wine again.

෨෬෩

ORDER OF THE BETROTHAL AND
MARRIAGE BLESSINGS

The officiating Rabbi holds a cup of wine and recites the following blessings:

בָּרוּךְ אַתָּה יְיָ אֱלֹהֵינוּ מֶלֶךְ הָעוֹלָם, בּוֹרֵא פְּרִי הַגָּפֶן:

בָּרוּךְ אַתָּה יְיָ אֱלֹהֵינוּ מֶלֶךְ הָעוֹלָם, אֲשֶׁר קִדְּשָׁנוּ בְּמִצְוֹתָיו וְצִוָּנוּ עַל
הָעֲרָיוֹת, וְאָסַר לָנוּ אֶת הָאֲרוּסוֹת, וְהִתִּיר לָנוּ אֶת הַנְּשׂוּאוֹת לָנוּ
עַל יְדֵי חֻפָּה וְקִדּוּשִׁין. בָּרוּךְ אַתָּה יְיָ, מְקַדֵּשׁ עַמּוֹ יִשְׂרָאֵל עַל יְדֵי חֻפָּה
וְקִדּוּשִׁין:

The groom drinks of the wine, then the bride. The groom then betroths the bride with a ring and says:

הֲרֵי אַתְּ מְקֻדֶּשֶׁת לִי בְּטַבַּעַת זוֹ כְּדַת מֹשֶׁה וְיִשְׂרָאֵל:

The *ketubah* (marriage contract) is read, and the groom hands it to the bride. The cup is refilled, and the following blessings are recited:[1]

בָּרוּךְ אַתָּה יְיָ אֱלֹהֵינוּ מֶלֶךְ הָעוֹלָם, בּוֹרֵא פְּרִי הַגָּפֶן:

בָּרוּךְ אַתָּה יְיָ אֱלֹהֵינוּ מֶלֶךְ הָעוֹלָם, שֶׁהַכֹּל בָּרָא לִכְבוֹדוֹ:

בָּרוּךְ אַתָּה יְיָ אֱלֹהֵינוּ מֶלֶךְ הָעוֹלָם, יוֹצֵר הָאָדָם:

בָּרוּךְ אַתָּה יְיָ אֱלֹהֵינוּ מֶלֶךְ הָעוֹלָם, אֲשֶׁר יָצַר אֶת הָאָדָם בְּצַלְמוֹ,
בְּצֶלֶם דְּמוּת תַּבְנִיתוֹ, וְהִתְקִין לוֹ מִמֶּנּוּ בִּנְיַן עֲדֵי עַד: בָּרוּךְ
אַתָּה יְיָ, יוֹצֵר הָאָדָם:

שׂוֹשׂ תָּשִׂישׂ וְתָגֵל הָעֲקָרָה, בְּקִבּוּץ בָּנֶיהָ לְתוֹכָהּ בְּשִׂמְחָה: בָּרוּךְ אַתָּה
יְיָ, מְשַׂמֵּחַ צִיּוֹן בְּבָנֶיהָ:

שַׂמֵּחַ תְּשַׂמַּח רֵעִים הָאֲהוּבִים, כְּשַׂמֵּחֲךָ יְצִירְךָ בְּגַן עֵדֶן מִקֶּדֶם: בָּרוּךְ
אַתָּה יְיָ, מְשַׂמֵּחַ חָתָן וְכַלָּה:

בָּרוּךְ אַתָּה יְיָ אֱלֹהֵינוּ מֶלֶךְ הָעוֹלָם, אֲשֶׁר בָּרָא שָׂשׂוֹן וְשִׂמְחָה, חָתָן
וְכַלָּה, גִּילָה רִנָּה דִּיצָה וְחֶדְוָה, אַהֲבָה וְאַחֲוָה שָׁלוֹם וְרֵעוּת,
מְהֵרָה יְיָ אֱלֹהֵינוּ יִשָּׁמַע בְּעָרֵי יְהוּדָה וּבְחוּצוֹת יְרוּשָׁלַיִם, קוֹל שָׂשׂוֹן
וְקוֹל שִׂמְחָה, קוֹל חָתָן וְקוֹל כַּלָּה, קוֹל מִצְהֲלוֹת חֲתָנִים מֵחֻפָּתָם,
וּנְעָרִים מִמִּשְׁתֵּה נְגִינָתָם: בָּרוּךְ אַתָּה יְיָ, מְשַׂמֵּחַ חָתָן עִם הַכַּלָּה:

The groom, then the bride drink from the wine again.

---

1. At the conclusion of the Blessing After a Meal, the blessing over the wine is recited after the following six blessings.

BIBLIOGRAPHY

BIBLIOGRAPHY

Asher Bara, 5689: Chasidic Discourse delivered by Rabbi Yosef Yitzchak Schneersohn, sixth Lubavitcher Rebbe, on 14 Kislev 5689 (1928). (Heb.)

Avodah Zarah: Talmudic tractate discussing the subject of idolatry.

Avot d'Rabbi Natan: Commentary on Avot, by the Babylonian sage, Rabbi Natan, printed in all standard editions of the Talmud.

Berachot: Talmudic tractate discussing the laws of blessings.

Bereishit Rabbah: See *Midrash Rabbah.*

Biurei Hazohar: Chasidic expositions on the *Zohar* and the *Tikkunei Zohar* by Rabbi Menachem Mendel Schneersohn, third Lubavitcher Rebbe, the "Tzemach Tzedek;" two volumes. (Heb.)

B'shaah Shehikdimu 5672: Series of discourses delivered by Rabbi Shalom DovBer Schneersohn, fifth Lubavitcher Rebbe, during the years 5672-5676 (1912-1915), named for its opening phrase; three volumes. (Heb.)

Chacham Tzvi (Responsa): Responsa by R. Tzvi Hirsch Ashkenazi (1656-1718. First published in Amsterdam, 1712. (Heb.)

Derech Chaim: Classic work by R. DovBer, second Lubavitcher Rebbe, on *teshuvah* and Divine service. Kopust, 1819; Brooklyn, NY, 1955; 2002. (Heb.)

Derech Mitzvotecha: Work by Rabbi Menachem Mendel Schneersohn, third Lubavitcher Rebbe, the "Tzemach Tzedek," offering Chasidic explanations for certain *mitzvot.* Also known as *Ta'amei Hamitzvot.* (Heb.)

Derushei Chatunah: Collection of Chasidic discourses delivered by Rabbi Yosef Yitzchak Schneersohn, sixth Lubavitcher Rebbe, on the occasion of the wedding of his daughter, Rebbetzin Chaya Mushka, to Rabbi Menachem M. Schneerson. (Heb.)

Dikdukei Sofrim: Collection of alternate versions of the Talmud found in manuscripts and early printed editions, by Rabbi Rafael Nattan Natta Rabinowitz. 15 vol., Munich, 1868-1886.

Eichah Rabbah: See *Midrash Rabbah*.

Eitz Chaim: A compilation of the Arizal's Kabbalistic teachings, by his primary disciple and exponent, Rabbi Chaim Vital (1543-1620).

Forces in Creation: English translation of *Yechayenu Miyomayim 5659*, delivered by the fifth Lubavither Rebbe, R. Shalom DovBer Schneersohn, on Rosh Hashanah 5659 (1898) (Kehot, 2003).

Four Worlds, The: English translation of a letter by Rabbi Yosef Yitzchak Schneersohn, sixth Lubavitcher Rebbe, explaining the mystical worlds of *Atzilut, Beriah, Yetzirah*, and *Asiyah* (Kehot, 2003).

Hayom Yom: Anthology of aphorisms and customs arranged according to the days of the year; assembled by the Lubavitcher Rebbe, Rabbi Menachem M. Schneerson, from the talks and writings of his father-in-law, Rabbi Yosef Y. Schneersohn. (New York, 1943, Heb./Yid.)

Ibn Ezra: Commentary on the Torah by R. Avraham Ibn Ezra (1080-1164) of Spain, expert grammarian, philosopher, astronomer, mathematician, doctor and poet. Naples, 1488; Constantinople, 1522.

Iggeret Hakodesh: A selection of letters by R. Schneur Zalman of Liadi dealing with such topics as charity, prayer, and the like. Fourth part of *Tanya*.

Keter Shem Tov: A collection of teachings of R. Yisrael Baal Shem Tov, culled from the writings of his students. Zalkava, 1794; New York, 1973; 1999. Revised edition, New York, 2004.

Ketubot: Talmudic tractate discussing marriage contracts.

L'chol tichlah, 5659: Chasidic discourse delivered by Rabbi Shalom DovBer Schneersohn, fifth Lubavitcher Rebbe, on Shabbat Parshat Vayera, 5659 (1898). (Heb.)

Lecha Dodi, 5689: Chasidic discourse delivered by Rabbi Yosef Yitzchak Schneersohn, sixth Lubavitcher Rebbe, on 14 Kislev 5689 (1928). (Heb.)

Lecha Dodi, 5714: Chasidic discourse delivered by the Lubavitcher Rebbe, Rabbi Menachem M. Schneerson on 13 Elul 5714 (1954). (Heb.)

Likkutei Torah: A collection of discourses elucidating major themes of Leviticus, Numbers, Deuteronomy, Song of Songs, Pesach, Shavuot, the High Holidays and Sukkot according to Chasidic philosophy. Delivered by the founder of Chabad Chasidus, Rabbi Schneur Zalman of Liadi, they were published in 5608 (1848) by his grandson Rabbi Menachem Mendel Schneersohn, third Lubavitcher Rebbe, the "Tzemach Tzedek." (Heb.)

Likkutei Torah L'gimmel Parshiot: Discourses on Bereshit, Noach and Lech Lecha from *Torah Or* by R. Schneur Zalman of Liadi, with notes by R. Menachem Mendel Schneersohn, third Lubavitcher Rebbe, the "Tzemach Tzedek," and R. Shmuel, fourth Lubavitcher Rebbe. Vilna, 1884. (Heb.)

Maamarei Amdur Ha'emtzaei: Chasidic discourses by R. DovBer, second Lubavitcher Rebbe. 19 vol., Brooklyn, NY, 1985-1992.

Maamarei Admur Hazaken: Chasidic discourses by R. Schneur Zalman of Liadi. 24 vol., Brooklyn, NY, 1956-1995.

Midrash Rabbah: A major collection of homilies and commentaries on the Torah and the Five Megillot, attributed to Rabbi Oshaya Rabbah (circa. 3rd century); some place it as a work of the early Gaonic period.

Or Hatorah: Chasidic discourses on Scripture by R. Menachem Mendel of Lubavitch, the Tzemach Tzedek. Berditchev, 1913; Brooklyn, NY, 1950 and on.

Or Torah: A compilation of Chasidic teachings by Rabbi DovBer, the Maggid of Mezritch, leader of the second generation of Chasidism. Compiled by his students, this work provides unique insight into various concepts contained in Scripture, Talmud, and Kabbalah, through the Chasidic lens. First printed in Koretz, 5564 (1804). New, revised edition, Brooklyn, NY, 2006. (Heb.)

Overcoming Folly: A comprehensive treatise, by Rabbi Shalom DovBer Schneersohn, fifth Lubavitcher Rebbe. Written in the spirit and style of traditional ethical Torah teachings, it touches upon the various challenges one experiences when faced with the reality of material existence—obstacles that stand in the way of achieving true spiritual heights. Brooklyn, NY, 2006. (Hebrew: *Kuntres Umaayan*, Brooklyn, NY 1943.)

Pardes (Pardes Rimonim): Kabbalistic work by R. Moshe Cordovero (Ramak) of Safed (1522-1570), leader of a prominent Kabbalistic school in Safed.

Pesachim: Talmudic tractate discussing the Passover laws.

Rabbeinu Chananel: Rabbi Chananel ben Chushiel (c. 990-1050 ce), author of a commentary found in standard editions of the Talmud, believed to transmit many of the traditional interpretations of the Babylonian *Gaonim* to the newly emerging academies of the West.

Ramaz: Rabbi Moshe Zacuto (Amsterdam, 1625-Venice, 1697). A famous Rabbi and Kabbalist, he authored many works, including a commentary on the *Zohar*, printed in most editions.

Rashi: Acronym for Rabbi Shlomo Yitzchaki. Rabbi Shlomo ben Yitzchak lived in Troyes, France and Worms, Germany (1040-1105). His commentary is printed in practically all editions of the Torah and Talmud, and is the subject of some two hundred commentators.

Reshit Chochmah: Classic ethical work by Rabbi Eliyahu de Vidas, disciple of Rabbi Moshe Cordovero; completed in 1575.

Rosh Hashanah: Talmudic tractate discussing the laws of the Rosh Hashanah festival and the Jewish calendar.

Samach Tesamach, 5657: Series of Chasidic discourses delivered by R. Shalom DovBer Schneersohn, fifth Lubavitcher Rebbe, in 5657 (1897), on the occasion of the marriage of his son, Rabbi Yosef Yitzchak. (Heb.)

Mystical Concepts in Chasidism: Guide to the intricate concepts of Jewish mysticism found in Chabad Chasidic philosophy. Authored by Rabbi J. Immanuel Schochet (Kehot, 1988). (Eng.)

Sefer Hamaamarim 5643-5680: Set of Chasidic discourses delivered by Rabbi Shalom DovBer Schneersohn, fifth Lubavitcher Rebbe, between 5643-5680 (1883-1920), the years of his leadership; twenty-five volumes. (Heb.)

Sefer Hamaamarim 5680-5710: Set of Chasidic discourses delivered by Rabbi Yosef Yitzchak Schneersohn, sixth Lubavitcher Rebbe, between 5680-5710 (1920-1950), the years of his leadership; nineteen volumes. (Heb.)

Sefer Hamaamarim Kuntresim: Chasidic discourses delivered by Rabbi Yosef Yitzchak Schneersohn, sixth Lubavitcher Rebbe, from 5688 to 5710 (1928-1950). (Three volumes; Heb.)

Sefer Yetzirah: One of the oldest written sources of Kabbalah, it is attributed to the Patriarch Abraham. It has been the subject of over one hundred commentaries since it was first published in Mantua, 1562.

Semuchim La'ad, 5680: Chasidic discourse delivered by Rabbi Shalom DovBer Schneersohn, fifth Lubavitcher Rebbe, on 20 Marcheshvan 5680 (1919). (Heb.)

Shaar Hamitzvot: A compilation of the Arizal's Kabbalistic teachings on the commandments, by his primary disciple and exponent, Rabbi Chaim Vital (1543-1620). Salonika, 1856.

Shaar Hayichud v'haEmunah: Second part of Tanya; explores the doctrines of Divine Unity, Providence and faith; twelve chapters.

Shabbat: Talmudic tractate discussing the laws of Shabbat.

Shaloh: A monumental work by Rabbi Yeshayah Horowitz, (1558-1628), chief rabbi of Prague. Also known by its acronym, *Shelah*, it contains explanations and commentaries on the profound aspects of the Torah, *mitzvot*, the festivals, Jewish customs and the fundamental beliefs of Judaism, including basic instruction in Kabbalah. First published in Amsterdam, 1648.

She'elot u'Teshuvot Chacham Tzvi: See *Chacham Tzvi (Responsa).*

Shemot Rabbah: See *Midrash Rabbah.*

Shulchan Aruch Harav: Code of Jewish law by R. Schneur Zalman of Liadi. Shklov, 1814; Brooklyn, NY, 1960-8; 1999-2004.

Siddur im Dach: Lit., "Siddur with Chasidus." Also known as *Seder Tefillot Mikol Hashanah* (The Order of the Prayers of the Entire Year). Prayer book containing rulings and Chasidic discourses pertaining to the prayers by Rabbi Schneur Zalman of Liadi. (Heb.)

Siddur Tehillat Hashem: Prayer book according to the text of Rabbi Schneur Zalman of Liadi, first published in New York, 1945, and reprinted many times since.

Sukkah: Talmudic tractate discussing the festival of Sukkot and its laws.

Taanit: Talmudic tractate discussing fast days.

Tanchuma: Early *Midrash* on the Torah, attributed to R. Tanchuma bar Abba. Constantinople, 1522.

Tanya: Philosophical *magnum opus* by Rabbi Schneur Zalman of Liadi, in which the principles of Chabad are expounded. The name is derived from the initial word of this work. Also called *Likkutei Amarim.*

Tikkunei Zohar: A work of seventy chapters on the first word of the Torah, by the school of Rabbi Shimon bar Yochai (circa. 120 c.e.). First printed in Mantua, 1558, *Tikkunei Zohar* contains some of the most important discussions in *Kabbalah*, and is essential for understanding the *Zohar.*

Torah Or: A collection of discourses elucidating major themes of the weekly Torah portion and Festivals according to Chassidic philosophy. Delivered by the founder of Chabad Chasidus, Rabbi Schneur Zalman of Liadi (1745-1812), they were published by his grandson Rabbi Menachem Mendel of Lubavitch, the Tzemach Tzedek (1789-1866). (Heb.)

Torat Chaim: A collection of discourses elucidating major themes of the Torah portions of Bereishit-Pekudei, by Rabbi DovBer of Lubavitch. Kopust, 1886; Brooklyn NY, 1974; 2003. (Heb.)

Torat Menachem—Hitva'aduyot: Unedited talks of the Lubavitcher Rebbe, Rabbi Menachem M. Schneerson, spanning the years 5710-5720 and 5742-5752; seventy volumes. (Heb.)

Torat Shmuel 5626-5640: Set of Chasidic discourses delivered by Rabbi Shmuel Schneersohn, fourth Lubavitcher Rebbe, between 5626-5640 (1866-1880), the years of his leadership [5626-5643 (1866-1882)]; twenty-three volumes. (Heb.)

Transforming the Inner Self: English translation of the discourse beginning *Adam Ki Yakriv*, from *Likkutei Torah,*

Vayikra, delivered by R. Schneur Zalman of Liadi in 5572 (1812) (Kehot, 2004).

V'haya Ki Tavo, 5675: Chasidic discourse delivered by Rabbi Shalom DovBer Schneersohn, fifth Lubavitcher Rebbe, on Shabbat Parshat Tavo, 5675 (1915). (Heb.)

Yalkut Shimoni: One of the most popular early collections of Midrashic material, compiled by Rabbi Shimon Ashkenazi HaDarshan, a preacher in Frankfurt (circa. 1260). Many Midrashim are known only because they are cited in this work, first published in Salonika, 1521-27.

Yevamot: Talmudic tractate discussing levirate marriage.

Yom Tov Shel Rosh Hashanah 5666: Series of discourses delivered by Rabbi Shalom DovBer Schneersohn, fifth Lubavitcher Rebbe, during the years 5666-7 (1905-7), named for its opening words.

Zohar: Lit., "Radiance," this basic work of Kabbalah was compiled by Rabbi Shimon Bar Yochai (second century Mishnaic sage) as a commentary on the Torah. (Heb./Aram.)

Zohar Chadash: Additions to the *Zohar, Midrash Hane'elam* and *Tikkunei Zohar*. Includes *Zohar* on Song of Songs, Lamentations and *Midrash Rut*. (Heb.)

INDEX

INDEX

TITLES IN THE
CHASIDIC HERITAGE SERIES

THE ETERNAL BOND
FROM TORAH OR

Translated by Rabbi Ari Sollish

This discourse explores the spiritual significance of *brit milah*, analyzing two dimensions in which our connection with G-d may be realized. For in truth, there are two forms of spiritual circumcision. Initially, man must "circumcise his heart," freeing himself to the best of his ability from his negative, physical drives; ultimately, though, it is G-d who truly liberates man from his material attachment.

JOURNEY OF THE SOUL
FROM TORAH OR

Translated by Rabbi Ari Sollish

Drawing upon the parallel between Queen Esther's impassioned plea to King Ahasuerus for salvation and the soul's entreaty to G-d for help in its spiritual struggle, this discourse examines the root of the soul's exile, and the dynamics by which it lifts itself from the grip of materialism and ultimately finds a voice with which to express its G-dly yearnings. Includes a brief biography of the author.

TRANSFORMING THE INNER SELF
FROM LIKKUTEI TORAH

Translated by Rabbi Chaim Zev Citron

This discourse presents a modern-day perspective on the Biblical command to offer animal sacrifices. Rabbi Schneur Zalman teaches that each of us possesses certain character traits that can be seen as "animalistic," or materialistic, in nature, which can lead a person toward a life of material indulgence. Our charge, then, is to "sacrifice" and transform the animal within, to refine our animal traits and utilize them in our pursuit of spiritual perfection.

KNOWLEDGE AND FAITH

FROM LIKKUTEI TORAH

Translated by Rabbi Eli Kaminetzky

As true as the fact that the mind and its elements are gifts from G-d, so does faith inspire us in a way that mere accumulation of knowledge cannot. Faith's inspiration lifts us beyond the boundaries of our finite existence, yet, that inspiration can depart just as easily as it came. Knowledge, however, becomes a part of us and thus changes us decisively. In effect, faith and knowledge complement and balance each other. This discourse discusses the fundamental concept of faith in G-d as compared to the imperative to "know" G-d, and the differences between the two.

RABBI DOVBER OF LUBAVITCH

FLAMES

FROM SHAAREI ORAH

Translated by Dr. Naftoli Loewenthal

This discourse focuses on the multiple images of the lamp, the oil, the wick and the different hues of the flame in order to express profound guidance in the Divine service of every individual. Although *Flames* is a Chanukah discourse, at the same time, it presents concepts that are of perennial significance. Includes the first English biography of the author ever published.

RABBI MENACHEM MENDEL OF LUBAVITCH, THE TZEMACH TZEDEK

THE MITZVAH TO LOVE YOUR FELLOW AS YOURSELF

FROM DERECH MITZVOTECHA

Translated by Rabbis Nissan Mangel and Zalman I. Posner

The discourse discusses the Kabbalistic principle of the "collective soul of the world of *Tikkun*" and explores the essential unity of all souls. The discourse develops the idea that when we connect on a soul level, we can love our fellow as we love ourselves; for in truth, we are all one soul. Includes a brief biography of the author.

THE ART OF GIVING
FROM OR HATORAH

Translated by Rabbi Shmuel Simpson
Edited by Rabbi Avraham D. Vaisfiche

What's the ideal way to give tzedakah? Specifically, is it best to give whatever we can at any given time regardless of the amount, or should we postpone our tzedakah giving until such time as we can afford to make a more sizable contribution? Or is neither approach necessarily preferable to the other? This discourse emphatically exclaims that, yes, it does indeed make a difference how we go about giving to tzedakah, because the experience of tzedakah is about so much more than meets the eye.

RABBI SHMUEL OF LUBAVITCH

TRUE EXISTENCE
MI CHAMOCHA 5629

Translated by Rabbis Yosef Marcus and Avraham D. Vaisfiche

This discourse revolutionizes the age-old notion of Monotheism, i.e., that there is no other god besides Him. Culling from Talmudic and Midrashic sources, the discourse makes the case that not only is there no other god besides Him, there is nothing besides Him—literally. The only thing that truly exists is G-d. Includes a brief biography of the author.

TRUE EXISTENCE
THE CHASIDIC VIEW OF REALITY

A Video-CD with Rabbi Manis Friedman

Venture beyond science and Kabbalah and discover the world of Chasidism. This Video-CD takes the viewer step-by-step through the basic Chasidic and Kabbalistic view of creation and existence. In clear, lucid language, Rabbi Manis Friedman deciphers these esoteric concepts and demonstrates their modern-day applications.

CHANNELING THE DIVINE
ITTA B'MIDRASH TILLIM
Edited by Rabbi Avraham D. Vaisfiche

The Bar Mitzvah, the day a Jewish boy turns thirteen, is a turning point in his life. He comes of age, becoming responsible for adher-ence to the *mitzvot*—and everyone celebrates. Chabad Chasidim mark this milestone by having the "Bar Mitzvah boy" publicly deliver a discourse, originally delivered by Rabbi Shalom DovBer Schneersohn, fifth Lubavitcher Rebbe, on the occasion of his Bar Mitzvah in 5634 (1873). Its main theme is the cosmic impact of performing the mitzvah of *tefillin*, and the special connection between this mitzvah and the age of Bar Mitzvah.

FEMININE FAITH
L'HAVIN INYAN ROSH CHODESH, 5640
Translated by Rabbi Shais Taub

When the Jews served the Golden Calf during their sojourn in the wilderness, says the Midrash, the women refused to join them. This discourse traces the roots of the feminine within the supernalrealms, and explores its relationship to women and how it translat-ed into their aversion for unholy and ungodly worship. Why are women more sensitive than men to G-d's role in earthly events and His mastery over Creation? The answer explores G-d's unity and immanence in the world, and the innate sensitivity that women posses to spirituality.

RABBI SHALOM DOVBER OF LUBAVITCH

DIVINE SPEECH
YOM TOV SHEL ROSH HASHANAH 5659 DISCOURSE ONE
Translated by Rabbis Yosef Marcus and Moshe Miller

The discourse explores the attribute of *malchut* and the power of speech while introducing some of the basic concepts of Chasidism and Kabbalah in a relatively easy to follow format. Despite its title and date of inception, the discourse is germane throughout the year. Includes a brief biography of the author.

FORCES IN CREATION

YOM TOV SHEL ROSH HASHANAH 5659 DISCOURSE TWO

Translated by Rabbis Moshe Miller and Shmuel Marcus

> A fascinating journey beyond the terrestrial, into the myriad spiritual realms that shape our existence. Rabbi Shalom DovBer systematically traces the origins of earth, Torah and souls, drawing the reader higher and higher into the mystical, cosmic dimensions that lie beyond the here and now, and granting a deeper awareness of who we are at our core.

THE POWER OF RETURN

YOM TOV SHEL ROSH HASHANAH 5659 DISCOURSE THREE

Translated by Rabbi Y. Eliezer Danzinger

> This discourse examines the inner workings of *teshuvah*, and explains how it is precisely through making a detailed and honest examination of one's character and spiritual standing—which inevitably leads one to a contrite and broken heart—that allows one to realize his or her essential connection with G-d.

OVERCOMING FOLLY

KUNTRES UMAAYAN MIBEIT HASHEM

Translated by Rabbi Zalman I. Posner

> In this classis ethico-philosophical work, Rabbi Shalom DovBer weaves Chasidic doctrine, Kabbalah thoughts, Biblical and Talmudic texts and candid insights into human frailties into a document structured and systematic, yet informal and personal—a text for study and meditation.

TRACT ON PRAYER
KUNTRES HATEFILLAH

Translated by Rabbi Y. Eliezer Danzinger

Tract on Prayer expounds on the concept of *tefillah*—prayer, as understood in Chabad Chasidic philosophy. Building on the Talmudic dictum that prayer constitutes the "service of the heart," *Tract on Prayer* captures the quintessence of *tefillah* as the vehicle for attaining attachment to G-d. It guides the worshiper in preparing for this divine service of the heart, setting out the role and dynamics of contemplation before and during prayer. *Tract on Prayer* also explores various Kabbalistic and Chasidic concepts.

THE SIMPLE SERVANT
UMIKNEH RAV 5666

Translated by Rabbi Yosef Marcus

This discourse elaborates upon three types of personalities with distinct approaches to Divine service: 1) The child of G-d, naturally committed; 2) The loyal servant of G-d, motivated by his appreciation of G-d; 3) The simple servant of G-d, driven by his acceptance of the yoke of Heaven. His apathy makes serving G-d difficult. Yet he does his work consistently because he is reaching beyond himself—overcoming his own nature.

ALL FOR THE SAKE OF HEAVEN
PADA BESHALOM 5668

Translated by Rabbi Zalman Abraham

Delivered on the Chasidic holiday of Yud Tet Kislev, the Nineteenth of Kislev, in the year 5668 (1907) and opening with the verse *Pada Beshalom Nafshi*, the discourse discusses the correct approach to mundane human activities, such as eating, drinking, and business dealings, so that these can be carried out truly for the sake of Heaven.

EXPLORING THE SOUL
V'CHOL ADAM 5679

Translated by Rabbi Shmuel Simpson

An analysis of the biblical verse which forbids any man from being present in the sanctuary when the High Priest entered to seek atonement. If, as the verse in Leviticus states: "No man shall be in the Tent of Meeting" at that time, how could the High Priest himself be present? By *exploring the soul*, its composition, and transcendent levels, the discourse explains how the High Priest, on Yom Kippur, ascended to the sublime level of "no man," thus granting him the permission and sanction to enter the Holy of Holies.

RABBI YOSEF YITZCHAK OF LUBAVITCH

THE PRINCIPLES OF EDUCATION AND GUIDANCE
KLALEI HACHINUCH VEHAHADRACHAH

Translated by Rabbi Y. Eliezer Danzinger

The Principles of Education and Guidance is a compelling treatise that examines the art of educating. In this thought-provoking analysis, Rabbi Yosef Yitzchak teaches how to assess the potential of any pupil, how to objectively evaluate one's own strengths, and how to successfully use reward and punishment—methods that will help one become a more effective educator.

THE FOUR WORLDS
FROM IGROT KODESH

Translated by Rabbis Yosef Marcus and Avraham D. Vaisfiche
Overview by Rabbi J. Immanuel Schochet

At the core of our identity is the desire to be one with our source, and to know the spiritual realities that give our physical life the transcendental importance of the Torah's imperatives. In this letter to a yearning Chasid, the Rebbe explains the mystical worlds of *Atzilut, Beriah, Yetzirah,* and *Asiyah.*

ONENESS IN CREATION
KOL HAMAARICH B'ECHAD 5690

Translated by Rabbi Y. Eliezer Danzinger

Said by Rabbi Yosef Yitzchak at the close of his 1930 visit to Chicago, this discourse explores the concept of Divine Unity as expressed in the first verse of the *Shema*. The discourse maintains that it is a G-dly force that perpetually sustains all of creation. As such, G-d is one with creation. And it is our study of Torah and performance of the mitzvot that reveals this essential oneness.

CREATION AND REDEMPTION
HACHODESH 5700

Translated by Rabbi Yosef Marcus

Tishrei celebrates Creation, the birth of the world, indicative of the natural order. Nissan commemorates the miraculous Exodus from Egypt, or the supernatural. In human terms, when struggling with the obfuscation of the natural, the key is to recognize the dimension where the limitations of the natural order do not exist. In fact, the physical exists only so that we may demonstrate how it too exposes the Divine truth. And when we recognize this, we can realize the supernatural even within the natural.

THE MAJESTIC BRIDE
LECHA DODI 5689 / 5714

Translated by Rabbis Ari Sollish and Avraham D. Vaisfiche

Customarily recited by a groom at the Kabbalat Panim reception, *Lecha Dodi* traces the Kabbalistic meaning of the order of the wedding ceremony, when first the guests welcome the groom, and then walk with the groom to welcome the bride, at which point the groom covers the bride's face with the veil. The discourse cites a number of examples and other situations where similar procedures occur, finally applying the reasoning to groom and bride to understand the Kabbalat Panim ceremony and the purpose of marriage.

RABBI MENACHEM M. SCHNEERSON,
THE LUBAVITCHER REBBE

ON THE ESSENCE OF CHASIDUS
KUNTRES INYANA SHEL TORAS HACHASIDUS

This landmark discourse explores the contribution of Chasidus to a
far deeper and expanded understanding of Torah. The Rebbe analyzes
the relationship Chasidus has with Kabbalah, the various dimensions
of the soul, the concept of Moshiach and the Divine attributes.

FULL DEVOTION
LO TIHYEH MESHAKELAH 5712

Translated by Rabbi Zalman Abraham

Referred to as a landmark discourse, delivered by the Rebbe barely
two years after ascending to the leadership of Chabad-Lubavitch, this
discourse is perhaps unique among all of the Rebbe`s teachings in the
sense that its message required a retooling of our conception of divine
service. It discusses the self-satisfaction that might result from our love
and awe of G-d, and that contemplating the fact that our days upon
earth need to be utilized to the fullest serves to remove any such feelings of satisfaction.

RECURRING EXODUS
BECHOL DOR VADOR—VEHECHERIM 5734

Translated by Rabbi Yehuda Altein

These two Chasidic discourses explore the deeper dimensions of the
Exodus, and teach how one can experience the transition from slav-
ery to freedom on a daily basis. More than just a geographical region,
"Egypt" represents any obstacle that limits our ability to be our real
selves and reach our true potential. When we succeed and break free
of our own limitations, we are liberated from own Egypt, and experience our own Exodus. For this sentiment to endure, we, too, must

"pass through the sea on dry land," which refers to bringing awareness of G-d even to areas where it had previously been concealed.

GARMENTS OF THE SOUL
A DAY OF STRENGTH

VAYISHLACH YEHOSHUA 5736
28 SIVAN 5749

Translated by Rabbis Yosef Marcus and Levi Friedman

Often what is perceived in this world as secondary is in reality most sublime. What appears to be mundane and inconsequential is often most sacred and crucial. Thus, at their source, the garments of the human, both physical and spiritual, transcend the individual.

THE UNBREAKABLE SOUL

MAYIM RABBIM 5738

Translated by Rabbi Ari Sollish

No matter how much one may be inundated with materialism, the flame of the soul burns forever. A discourse that begins with an unequivocal declaration, it speaks to one who finds pleasure in the material world, yet struggles to find spirituality in his or her life.

VICTORY OF LIGHT

TANU RABANAN MITZVAT NER CHANUKAH 5738

Translated by Rabbi Yosef Marcus

Even darkness has a purpose: to be transformed into light. This discourse explains how we can draw strength from the story of Chanukah for our battle with spiritual darkness, so that we, like the Macabees of old, may attain a *Victory of Light*.

THE PATH TO SELFLESSNESS
YEHUDAH ATAH 5738

Translated by Rabbi Shmuel Simpson

> Beginning with the words *Yehuda Atah*, the discourse examines the
> blessing which Yaakov blessed his fourth son, Yehuda, as compared to
> the blessings he gave his first three sons, Reuven, Shimon and Levi.
> Yaakov's sons embody distinctive forms of divine service, which cor-
> respond to distinct sections of the prayers of Shema and the Amidah.
> Using these distinctions, the discourse further derives lessons about
> the bond between the individual Jewish soul and G-d.

NURTURING FAITH
KUNTRES PURIM KATTAN 5752

Translated by Rabbi Yosef Marcus

> At its core, this discourse discusses the function of a *nassi*, a Jewish
> leader, who awakens within every single person the deepest part of the
> soul. Similar to Moses, the *nassi* inspires the person so that one's most
> basic faith in G-d leaves the realm of the abstract and becomes real.
> *Nurturing Faith* will cultivate your bond with the Rebbe's role as the
> Moses of our generation.

STAYING THE COURSE
A COLLECTION OF DISCOURSES BY THE CHABAD REBBES ON THE
INSEPARABLE BOND BETWEEN REBBE AND CHASID

Translated by Rabbi Shmuel Simpson

> Discussing various ways through which the Chasid can continue
> to nurture and renew this bond, the discourses presented in this
> work speak to the seasoned Chasid as well as those newly intro-
> duced to the Rebbe and his teachings.

There are many important manuscripts that are ready to go to press, but are waiting for a sponsor like you.

Please consider one of these opportunities and make an everlasting contribution to Jewish scholarship and Chasidic life.

For more information please contact:

THE CHASIDIC HERITAGE SERIES
770 Eastern Parkway
Brooklyn, New York 11213
Tel: 718.774.4000
editor@kehot.com